HARVARD DIARY

HARVARD DIARY

*Reflections on the
Sacred and the Secular*

Robert Coles

CROSSROAD • NEW YORK

1988

The Crossroad Publishing Company
370 Lexington Avenue, New York, N.Y. 10017

Printed in the United States of America

Library of Congress Cataloging-in-Publication Data

Coles, Robert.
    Harvard diary : reflections on the sacred and the secular / Robert
Coles.
        p.   cm.
    ISBN 0-8245-0885-8
    1. Spiritual life.   2. Christianity—20th century.   3. Coles,
Robert.   I. Title.
BV4501.2.C6423   1988
200—dc19   88-1502
                                                                   CIP

To Jane,
and to our sons,
Bob and Danny and Mike

Contents

Introduction

Often, as I wrote the essays in this book, I thought of my father and the way he spent part of Sunday afternoons when I was a child. He would put down some unlined white paper before himself on his desk, take his Parker pen in hand, and begin a long, reflective letter to his father, his sisters, his brother, all of whom lived in Yorkshire, England. Those letters were not only newsy. They were occasions for him to look inward, share his thoughts and concerns with others whose opinions he valued, whom he respected not only as blood kin, but spiritual kin. I still remember, as a matter of fact, Sunday afternoon, December 7, 1941. I was a boy of eleven, and he had just finished his letter. As was his wont, he showed it to his wife, then to us, my brother and me—a way of sharing thoughts on this side of the Atlantic, before sending them on their long journey across the sea (no air mail, then). Suddenly the phone rang. A friend of my mother's, a neighbor, had called to announce that we were at war. My father received the news sadly but stoically—even though he knew well what war can bring, having lost an older brother in the battle of Ypres during the First World War. (He fought in the English army.) My father's response: to sit down and write another page, to go with the earlier letter. I remember asking my mother why—the stubbornness of our dad's letter-writing response to life's events. Her response has stayed with me for over forty years: "Those letters are your father's way of keeping a diary—thinking about things and trying to make sense of them through the written word."

In 1981, when the editors of *New Oxford Review,* a magazine much interested in religious matters (and their connection to social, political and economic questions) asked me to write a monthly column, I recalled my mother's words, my father's periodic "diary"

1

in the form of a letter. I recalled, too, his great admiration for George Orwell, a respect and affection that definitely preceded the post-war notorieties of *Animal Farm* and (in 1948) *1984*—after which a respected but far from famous pseudonymous writer, George Orwell, became, simply, Orwell. Dad loved George Orwell's "London Letters," which appeared in *Partisan Review;* he read that magazine *for* those dispatches, cutting them out, forthwith, and tossing out (too hastily, I fear) the rest of the magazine, meaning all sorts of fine essays. I can remember hearing his stodgy, Republican reason: "I'm tired of all those arguments on Marxism, pro and con." He liked the idea of getting to know a particular mind, as it tried to get to know itself through a series of penned communications, with the reader, as it were, sitting in as a friend, rather than as the primary person being addressed—a question of tone, obviously: whether one tries primarily to confront oneself, share oneself, as in a letter or a diary entry, or whether one is taking on one or another issue for a "them," the readers who are in the forefront of the mind as it does the work of setting down sentences.

I have tried for the former, hence the "diary" in the title of the column. I work at Harvard as a teacher, and so its presence in the title. I love working with the students, learning with them as I try to be a teacher—give lectures or be the leader of a seminar. I especially love talking with certain students who come to my office for an old-fashioned bull session: what the devil does this life mean, and how the devil ought we try to live it? As I get caught in such discussions, I remember similar struggles waged by my parents—by my father, in those letters he wrote, by my mother in the margins of the novels she read, especially the Tolstoy ones. She loved him so, his wisdom as it gradually unfolded in the magic of his story-telling. In my own life I keep remembering my father, taking stock with the help of writers such as Orwell (or Dickens, or George Eliot), and my mother doing so through the after-thoughts Tolstoy provoked in her. I suspect that those memories persist not only in my head, but in the various pieces that have been published in recent years as "Harvard Diary."

More than anything, my parents struggled with moral questions, as did their literary heroes; and I have noticed that the writers I admire are similarly preoccupied—not with moral reasoning or philosophical analysis, but with the concrete particulars of everyday life which novelists know to render: our conduct, as each day tests it, rather than a host of hifalutin concepts—or as William Carlos Williams kept challenging us in *Paterson:* "no ideas but in things." Similarly with the children it's my job as a child psychiatrist to get to know: they grab at a morning's, an afternoon's earthy situations, maybe grubby moments, and try to come up with a point of view that will carry them along. Sometimes they, too, will write a few words down, in order to have a more lasting record of what has crossed their minds, as with this brief composition of an eight-year-old boy, trying hard to do a good job in the third grade of his school, a few miles away from Harvard: "We all behave sometimes. But sometimes we don't. When we don't, it is too bad."

Not all of us who have gone much further than he educationally are so alert morally—willing to say, flat out, that we regret our lapses; all too often we even manage not to acknowledge or notice them. The intellect can be a tricky ally—conceal as much as it reveals, uncovers. Worse, the intellect can fail in the moral sense— run roughshod over a particular world in an effort to be first at all costs. This competitive and solipsistic side of academic life, with all the attendant, endemic gossip and bad-mouthing, is an unfortunate commonplace—a reminder to all of us who teach and learn from one another in colleges and universities that moral virtues, to say the least, are not the inevitable reward of high academic performance. Once one has begun to notice such an irony—the college teacher who requires a bit of (moral) learning himself or herself— the writing of any number of novelists becomes newly suggestive. As I look back at many of the "diary entries" which are assembled here, I realize how hard I was struggling with that irony. No wonder I keep recalling a similar struggle in, say, James Agee or Orwell, William Carlos Williams or Tolstoy, Walker Percy or Flannery O'Connor: these writers can be penetrating, indeed, in their willingness to examine the confines of the intellect—the points where, as Emerson reminded us, character becomes the central issue. Much is often made of the stimulation a university provides, but I fear the above-mentioned spur to introspection is not always kept in mind by those of us who have rejoiced in the delights of our academic life.

In a sense, these essays have been occasions for me to learn about the assumptions which have informed my work—the values and ideals (and blind spots, too) I've carried around as I've talked with children here and abroad, tried to write about them, and as I've done my teaching, seen my patients. The reader will soon enough see that I am still loyal to many of my parents' values—their preference for novels and short stories as a means of moral and social (and yes, political) reflection—as opposed to the social sciences, a contemporary addiction of ours in late 20th century America. I bring to these essays my favorite writers—whose books are companions, and whose worries and hopes, worked into stories or clear and compelling narrative prose, I keep presenting to students as worth attending closely. I also bring to the pages that follow portraits of certain people I've met—ordinary in their own way, yet ever so special: men, women and children, often quite humble or obscure, yet wonderfully knowing teachers, unforgettable human beings. I am glad that I was lucky to know a person such as Dorothy Day—but she would be the first to remind me, remind all of us, how much there is to learn from all sorts of others, who may not have many social or cultural advantages, but who have a keen eye, a sharp ear for hypocrisy, phoniness, self-importance, qualities not entirely lacking in university communities, among others.

I want to thank Dale Vree, the editor of *New Oxford Review,* for his patience with me and kindness to me. These essays would not have been written were it not for his suggestion that I write regularly for the magazine he has done so much to shape in recent years. As the reader will see, I have tried to share my personal views, my politics, my literary enthusiasms, my experiences as I've done my research—I hope with some control over that "unreflecting egoism" George Eliot long ago warned us all to expect as a constant adversary. For the failures of vision or language in what follows, I take full responsibility—but, again, offer my thanks to Mr. Vree for his continual encouragement. I also thank Michael Leach for his warm interest in this book, his thoughtful attention to what I have written. Together we collected all the "Harvard Diary" pieces I'd done the past six years, cut only a few for the sake of a manageable book, and left intact the writing and the chronological order of the essays, on the assumption that they really have been diary entries by someone who happens to work at a university named Harvard.

A last, brief remark: a diary bespeaks of one's everyday life, its inevitable ups and downs, its victories and defeats. Lord, I thank You for the presence in my life of my wife Jane, and our children, Bob, Danny, Mike—and so, the dedication.

Remembering Dorothy Day

I first met Dorothy Day at a distance. In the 1950s I was a medical student, and much interested in getting away from the cloister of a decidedly academic experience in which patients were unfortunately becoming for me just a bundle of signs and symptoms. I was also struggling hard to connect a strong interest in moral philosophy to the work I was learning as a member of a particular profession—one supposedly close in its everyday preoccupations to what used to be called "ultimate concerns," many of which, alas, seem to be ardently pursued these days in courses called "psychological counseling" or "interviewing techniques." A visit to a Catholic Worker "hospitality house," located in one of New York City's poorer districts, helped me enormously—bridged, a bit, an abstract interest with a concrete situation. There Dorothy Day was, freely acknowledging without embarrassment her own reasons for feeding and clothing the extremely needy—"the lame, the halt, the blind," as she often put it, thereby demonstrating a preference for a biblical rather than sociological language.

Eventually I came to know her; know her great kindness and her constant example of religious faith; know her almost uncanny mix of selfless devotion to the humble ones with wry detachment—as if her soul was in closest communion across time and space with Dostoyevski and Tolstoy, those two 19th-century Russian fellow Christians who meant so much to her, and whose books, I think it fair to say without the slightest exaggeration, haunted her every day of her life. One day, she permitted me to scribble some notes as she talked; another time, I took with me a tape recorder, virtually a venerated instrument of a pagan faith (social science). I was bothering her with my confusions and curiosities, much of them centered on what I took to be her "inconsistency"—a radical political life, a

5

conservative religious one. She wanted no part of the distinction: "I don't act politically on the street or worship in church in order to fit in with people who are 'radical,' or people who are 'conservative.' I read the Bible. I try to pay attention to the life of Jesus Christ, our Lord. I try to follow His example. I stumble all the time, but I try to keep going—along the road He walked for us. I am a Catholic, of course; I belong to a Church, and when I made the decision to join it, I knew my whole life would change. For me, everything is religious—politics and the family and work, they all are part of our obligation: to follow our Lord's way."

She was, as she herself put it, "a fool for Christ." She was an utterly devout Catholic who, with Bernanos and Mauriac, knew that the Church today will falter, will fail in its mission, will become badly flawed—and yet, is a chosen instrument of His. Even as Judas once betrayed Him, the clergy now do, and parishioners now do—man's sinful nature. Still, there is hope—and Dorothy Day knew where to look for it: not in the pagan state; not in the dreary banalities and faddish abstractions of social science; not in the cultivation of self; not in a rampant, crazy consumerism; but in the daily struggle to obey God and live a life that does as much justice as possible to His constantly demonstrated lovingkindness. "All the way to Heaven is Heaven," she observed, again and again, quoting Catherine of Siena, who added, "because He said, 'I am the Way.'" Her life, then, gave us a glimpse of Heaven—we who have to live with the knowledge that Hell has a far larger claim on our journey than on that of Dorothy Day.

April 1981

The Loss Is a Gain

He was born in Atlanta, Georgia, during Dwight Eisenhower's second term. His parents were Georgia tenant farmers who had given up, finally, and moved to the city in desperation and hope. They left behind their own parents, who were the great-grand-children of slaves. No one in the family had ever gotten much of an education, let alone graduated from high school—until he did, in early May of 1975. My wife and I knew an uncle of his, who had, in fact, taken part in the civil rights movement of the 1960s, so we were invited to the ceremony, and attended. Even before we had met him we were told by his proud uncle that he had been admitted to "one of the fanciest northern colleges there is." I was afraid to ask the question; my wife did—and we thereupon had a discussion about Yale University in New Haven, Connecticut, and how fancy, indeed, it could be there. We both invited the young man to look us up when it came to be his turn to venture even further north, to explore, savor, take the measure of yet additional fancy terrain.

I think I came to know him fairly well in the course of those occasional forays. His uncle really did press him to come see me, and we got on fairly well. I showed him the various Harvard buildings here in Cambridge, Massachusetts, and I told him what I was then trying to accomplish—make sense of the work I'd done, studying for 20 years the ways different kinds of children, in various parts of the country, grow up and develop particular hopes and worries and fears. The more we talked, the more he remembered his own childhood; and the more we talked the more he pressed me about the kind of adulthood we both shared—as members of similar communities, whose moral and social contours he was anxious to survey: "When I was a boy I was told to believe in God; I was told that He was watching over us all the time, and if you have

7

any questions, He's the one, in the end, to go see. Of course, you never see Him; you pray to him, and He answers you 'in the Spirit'—that's a phrase my grandmother always used. Now I'm up here, though, and I'm studying all these 'subjects,' and everyone who writes a book knows the answer, and the teachers know the answer, and we think we know the answer. Us Yalies, the Harvard students, we think *we're* the answer, to be blunt.

"I go home—not to Atlanta (that's a place of convenience), but to Fitzgerald, Georgia, where my grandparents still live, and I'm with my people again. I'm not with some sociologist's *idea* of my people, or an economist's *idea* of how they live, or a psychologist's *interpretation* of their 'attitudes'; I'm with each and every one of *them,* my kin. I'm in church and that means half of Sunday, and plenty of times during the week: the praying out loud; the singing at the top of your voice, with your heart open full and right out there on your sleeve; the heads nodding *yes* or the heads shaking *no* back and forth; the speaking out, the testifying, the direct words sent to God; the listening—much more carefully than anyone does in Yale's lecture halls; the singing, oh yes, the singing—the field songs and the blues music and the gospel songs, our people trying with all their might to catch God's ear, coax Him to hear us, maybe beg Him for mercy, maybe soothe *His* nerves. I remember my grandmother saying: 'It ain't no good, no siree, for us to be asking of Him, always the asking. We have to think of *Him*—all of us, each of us, the millions over the world on their knees with wishes and worries.' As I got older I tried to tell her that God could take care of Himself, because He's God. But to my grandmother, God is always (partially, I guess) Christ on the Cross, *suffering*—for us! And up here, at Harvard and Yale, He's—well, He's nowhere! Up here, everyone is fighting it out—the battles are 'mean and hard,' as we'd say back home—and what they're fighting for is: themselves! To be a god! Each one wants his believers and followers."

A bit bitter, one notices at the time. Possibly a bit unfair, as well. And then come the secular social science weapons that, in the clutch, are available for such occasions: This poor fellow, trying to "bridge two cultures"; trying to "cope" with his various "problems," among them, no doubt, "feelings of inadequacy"; trying, as well, to deal with all sorts of "socioeconomic issues," not to mention a few of our other contemporary hyphenated ones—psychohistorical, psycho-sexual. And on and on the dreary, overwrought banalities go. "It's hard for them," I heard an ever so compassionate, proudly liberal Ivy League teacher say—in connection with youths such as the one quoted above. I asked for some specifics, and got a mouthful of pieties—talk of psychiatric "stages" and cultural "phases" and historical "contexts," lots and lots of earnest efforts at explaining, always explaining this life's various events. ("The task of the novelist," said Flannery O'Connor, "is to deepen mystery.")

Why not explain? That is what Yale and Harvard (or at least certain precincts of them) are justifiably all about. But a young Georgian gone North had begun to realize that a lot more was happening in that temporary Connecticut residence than "the pursuit of learning," pure if not so simple—even as his own ancestral home was not quite what he was being asked to believe it was by an assortment of "experts," including some whose skin was as dark as his. On that last score he would eventually become rather outspoken, even vehement: "All those urban-studies authorities and rural-studies authorities, all these people full of *ideas*—about the black personality and black culture and black history and black this and black that. They're doing to us what they do to the white man (equal justice under the law!). They're dissecting us, analyzing us, folding us into their theories. They're changing the way we think about ourselves. But they miss the most important thing: our soul. I don't mean 'soul food'; I don't even mean 'soul music.' (Everyone is on to those!) I mean my grandmother in church, calling to Jesus, loving Jesus, making that connection, everyday of her life, making it, between His life and hers, and believing in Him, in His love, in His compassion, in the grace He offered to us, to my grandmother and to millions of others like her. It was the black church that gave audience after audience to Dr. King, the same black church that became an embarrassment to lots of black and white activists— something to be interpreted away, called names, put aside, replaced. Replaced by what? Black power? Black psychology? Black studies? I cringe sometimes: I know all I've gained up here, but there will be some days when I feel the loss deep inside, and I want with all my heart and soul to go back and sit with my grandmother and pray to Him, the God Almighty of my memory."

December 1981

Psychiatric Stations of the Cross

Some months ago I visited a medical school classmate of mine in a first-rate Boston teaching hospital. He was (is still) seriously ill. Cancer will eventually take him, he knows. He has always been a rather quiet and thoughtful person—a stoic temperamentally. But he is also a deeply religious man; he attends a suburban Catholic church every Sunday, and on certain weekdays tries to set aside an hour or so for one of the Masses offered in a downtown chapel. When I came to see him he would have no part, from the very start, of any usual conversation. He was angry, and quite ready to tell me why. A priest had just come by, and indicated a strong interest in how the doctor/patient was managing to "cope." My friend said he was doing "fine" the way (he assumed) any of us has the right to say "fine." That is, he meant to indicate he was getting along reasonably well, given a particular predicament; *and* he had no great wish, at that moment, to elaborate on the matter in any detail.

For the visiting clergyman, however, such asserted poise and reticence were not to be accepted at face value. The priest persisted in asking questions which, in sum, amounted to a relentless kind of psychological inquiry. How was the patient "feeling"? How was his "spirit"? (These days, alas, such a word has lost its religious significance for all too many of us.) How was he "managing," in view of the "stress" he had to "confront"? Did he want to "talk about" what was happening? Were there any "thoughts" he might want to "bring up for discussion"?

The priest no doubt believed himself to be tactful, respectful, and considerate, but my friend was annoyed at the time of the visit, and a few hours later, quite enraged. He had wanted to talk with the priest about God and His ways, about Christ's life and death, about the Gospel of Luke (a particular favorite), about Heaven and

Hell—only to be approached repeatedly with psychological words and phrases. In their entirety those words and phrases constituted a statement, an insinuation: you are in psychological jeopardy, and that is what I, an ordained priest of the Holy Roman Catholic Church, have learned to consider more important than anything else, when in the presence of a person such as you.

To the patient such an attitude, such a *faith*, really, put into practice, was an outrageously gratuitous and arrogant affront: "He comes here with a Roman collar, and offers me psychological banalities as God's word!" I tried to be a bit "understanding," as it is put, tried to say that the priest meant well. But my friend was not about to let *that*, of all remarks, go by unchallenged. The priest certainly didn't "mean well," I was told. The priest was a "fool," was yet another apostate from the Christian religion. The priest was mesmerized by the mind and its commonplace workings—when he was supposed to be a man of The Book, alert to matters *sub specie aeternitatis*.

Our conversation on this vexing subject lengthened. I found myself remembering all the letters I've written, over the years, to bishops in the Catholic Church or the Episcopal Church—certifying one person's or another's "mental stability" or "normality" or "psychological health." Had I ever known my fellow psychiatrists to ask the clergymen what they thought of the character, the moral make-up of this or that would-be doctor or psychiatric trainee? Put differently, why is it that psychiatry now has so much intellectual, and yes, moral authority among the clergy? Why are so many of us uncritical with regard to the endless willingness of so many in our society to use psychiatric concepts in a normative, if not self-righteous and moralistic manner? If one likes the person and his or her "behavior," one compliments him or her psychologically: "adaptive defense mechanisms," or a "healthy" way of "handling the problem." If one is not so friendly to a person, there are all sorts of names to hurl about: "sick," of course, or "pathological" or "disturbed," and dozens of others.

I do not mean to deny the value of clinical terms, only to indicate that they have become quite something else: a moral code strongly compelling not only to the laity, but the clergy—as in "pastoral counseling," which for all too many of us has become a religious calling, with the Bible and its various messages as anecdotal adjuncts, quaint leftovers from an earlier era. I recently read a description of the background and qualifications of an Episcopal parish's newly-appointed minister and, I swear, almost all the statements pertained to his various secular interests and experience—in schools and hospital clinics and various social or political causes. I wish to emphasize that I do not have anything against a minister (or anyone else) choosing to devote time and effort to the sick and the poorly educated, or to a given set of community, not to mention national, concerns. The issue is something else—a matter, one speculates, for some at least, of self-respect: the priest happy and fulfilled as a psychologist or a social worker or a political activist, with his religious duties—his wonderful sacramental responsibilities!—turned into mere habits or social routines.

My doctor friend, unfortunately, lacked compassion for the particular priest mentioned above—or so he told me. Indeed, he had his Bible ready for the next priestly visit: "I'll wait for him to do his song and dance about my 'feelings'—and I'll watch him as he thinks to himself how smart he is, slowly probing and nudging me toward the discussion he is determined to have, at all costs! Suddenly, I interrupt him, pick up the Bible from the night table, and ask him to read from it—any part he wishes. He looks surprised and confused. He asks me if there is anything more I want to 'talk about.' I say no. I say I only want him to read from our Lord's Book. He does. He opens up the Bible and begins reading. He doesn't select a page, he just reads from the page that happens to be there: Psalm 69. Then he leaves, without saying much except he hopes I do well."

One soon enough reads Psalm 69: "Save me, O God; for the waters are come into my soul. I sink in deep mire, where there is no standing: I am come into deprivation, where the floods overflow me." There are, of course, many kinds of burdens in this life. I wonder whether the deepest mire, the deepest waters, for many of America's clergy, not to mention us laymen, may be found in the dreary solipsistic world so many of us have learned to find so interesting: the mind's moods, the various "stages" and "phases" of "human development" or of "dying," all dwelt upon (God save us!) as if Stations of the Cross.

January–February 1982

Mystery and Flannery O'Connor

In the teaching I do with college students and those at medical school, Flannery O'Connor's stories are especially edifying and suggestive. It is an unlikely encounter—a voice of unapologetic Catholic orthodoxy, a voice, too, of Southern 1950's social conservatism, heeded rather carefully by a significantly secular Yankee audience of 1980's youth. Of course, O'Connor was a marvelous storyteller, and a scrupulously careful writer, and so she can be (and often is) appreciated on predominantly aesthetic grounds—the intricate and suggestive symbolism, the shrewd use of humor, the disarming resort to a regional idiom or country piety, all in the service of a complex philosophical and theological presentation. Still, her stories, her two novels *(Wise Blood, The Violent Bear It Away)* are meant to be more than entertaining, or even edifying. They are, in sum, an insistent vision, whose essence has been spelled out for the reader of nonfiction in Miss O'Connor's *Mystery and Manners,* a collection of essays bristling with several kinds of truculent dissatisfaction.

For one thing, she was continually alert to the stupid arrogance of certain literary centers of influence: "I have found that anything that comes out of the South is going to be called grotesque by the Northern reader unless it is grotesque, in which case it is going to be called realistic." But unacknowledged parochialism, for her, was not only a matter of geography. She understood all too well the modern, agnostic, liberal sensibility of mid-20th century America. "The social sciences," she once observed, "have cast a dreary blight on the public approach to fiction." And not only fiction! Here she is, upon return from one of those college symposia which have become, for so many, ecclesiastical in significance: "Boy do I have a stomach full of liberal religion! The Devil had his day there. It

13

began with Boas talking about 'Art and Magic.' I don't know what he meant to say but he left the impression that religion was good because it was art and magic. Nothing behind it, but it's good for you."

The statement immediately above was written in a letter, which Sally Fitzgerald included in *The Habit of Being,* her selection and arrangement of O'Connor's side of a correspondence noteworthy for its very existence (in this age of the telephone and television), not to mention its singularly penetrating depth. In an essay titled "The Teaching of Literature," part of *Mystery and Manners,* Flannery (as one wants to call her, because she was so unpretentious, and because her particular first name has so much dignity to it, and is as rare as she was) throws down an even more direct challenge to—well, she tells us whom: "Not long ago a teacher told me that her best students feel it is no longer necessary to write anything. She said they think that everything can be done with figures now, and that what can't be done with figures isn't worth doing. I think this is a natural belief for a generation that has been made to feel that the aim of learning is to eliminate mystery. For such people, fiction can be very disturbing, for the fiction writer is concerned with mystery that is lived." One wants to qualify: *some* fiction, and *some* fiction writers! Her kind of storytelling, her angle of vision, really, was best described by a comment of hers elsewhere in the same essay: "It is the business of fiction to embody mystery through manners, and mystery is a great embarrassment to the modern mind."

She was a great one for showing, in her stories, what lots of us hold dear—in lieu of a respectful, humble awe. A story titled "The Lame Shall Enter First" offers a devastating critique of the modern "mental health professional" as a smug, self-obsessed shepherd. (The central character is named Sheppard.) She remembers the fourth chapter of Luke, of course: "Physician, heal thyself." She has taken stock of her fellow citizens—the hunger we have, persistent and insatiable, for one psychological cliche after another, for an apparently endless succession of sociological phrases, those explanatory "contexts" which seem to mesmerize us, until a stale taste prompts yet another menu to be held up as (finally) the one that will settle the stomach for good.

Illusions were her particular "area of expertise." (Lord, that phrase is everywhere and we have no preventative antitoxins!) She could spot instantly a deluded fact-monger, a self-important theorist full of blah—and very important, she could tell us what to make of our own credulity: the blind leading the blind, as in the Gadarene swine of the New Testament. Her shepherd is so busy trying to offer a "therapeutic approach" (as it is put all the time these days) he has not time left to examine his own assumptions, never mind extend a much needed hand of love to his own son. It is the old, sad paradox—those who denounce the "illusions" of others, are victim of their own kind of illusions, and those who offer all sorts of solutions and cures to patients, never mind entire nations, manage to exhibit, often enough unwittingly, the feet of clay which millions of ordinary men and women have never pretended to lack.

Put differently, Flannery O'Connor wondered about the secular messianic movements of this century; wondered about those who offer transcendence, while forgetting the large shadow that always follows us, the immanent reality of our everyday life, with all its moments of victory or defeat. For her, mystery is a gift of God; without it we have no choice but self-intoxication. Her "mystery," of course, had to do with the supernatural. She had no animus against science, against the boldest explorations of mind or matter—of people, places, things. She only wanted us to understand where the water's edge begins—at what point we are not exploring, but rather, imploring in our own name. In my own profession, Freud's example is, as usual, instructive: when he was analyzing mental behavior, he was marvelously knowing, and usually, rather tentative; when he wrote about religion he became bitter, preachy, and anxious to bow before *his* faith (science), while ridiculing everyone else's as a set of "illusions." Nor was he willing to examine the interesting way his ideas became what he himself described as a "movement," with rings given comrades, and "tenets" either upheld by "members," or expulsion the consequence.

For the Christian, needless to say, such a result serves as yet another reminder of how stubbornly pride clings to us, how hard it is to come by even a modest amount of humility—hence our need for forgiveness. In comparison, the word "cure" is so final; no acknowledgment that at each sunrise we must prepare to struggle with the same obstacles before us, and hope and pray and work for one hour's success, then another's, as we slouch (rather than ride in this or that theory's gilded chariot) toward Bethlehem.

March 1982

Christ and the Poor

In 1979 my son and I worked our way up the slopes of one of Rio de Janeiro's *favellas*. The higher one goes, the poorer the people—so that, ironically, in at least one beautiful coastal city, the least consequential of all families get to have the best of all views. The *favellas* begin near a road, and over the years, new families keep appearing; they climb their way up, past existing shacks, and begin building flimsy new ones. No electricity. No plumbing or heating. No water. No medical care. Death a constant companion to those of all ages. I remember my son and I trying hard to stifle the nausea and dizziness we felt—a response to the fetid smells which (for us) dominated a hot and lazy Monday afternoon.

From every point in the *favella* one could see a dramatic figure atop another of Rio's many hills: *Monumento de Cristo Redentor*, a monument to Christ, the redeemer. The children were anxious to tell us everything—that the name of the elevation was Corcovado Rock, that the statue was completed in October 1931. One girl, 12 years old, said this to my son: "My day begins when I go outside and look at Jesus. I tell Him good morning. My day ends when I say goodnight to Jesus. I am sure He wants everyone to sleep well. We are lucky He chose us to live! We'll be seeing Him soon! The nuns tell us He keeps His eyes out for the *favellados*."

My son, a few years older, couldn't forget that last observation. He wanted to know whether God does indeed have any special regard for one or another segment of the world's population—and he was not unaware of the Galilean sermons Jesus delivered almost 2,000 years ago. We decided to ask the question of the girl's mother, a fairly outgoing and reflective woman (for all the hardship and misery she had to confront, day in and day out). She was quick to reply: "Can you imagine Jesus Christ living in one of those buildings in Copacabana, or Iponema [where the rich of Rio live]? Can you imagine Him boasting that He owns many cars and boats, has lots of money in the bank, and owns a big house on the ocean, south of Rio, besides His apartment here? I clean for them, the big shots. I know how much they own. There is only one piece of property they don't own: Heaven! They can't buy it, even with the millions and millions of *cruzeiros* [Brazil's monetary unit] you hear them mentioning all the time. God came to us as a poor man, the nuns say, and that must mean a lot! I tell my children that they would live better if they'd been born luckier, born to a Copacabana businessman. But that is one life; there are *two* lives we have to think about: this life and another life to come."

I doubt the most sophisticated theologian could put the matter much better. Christ chose to be a migrant preacher who paid constant attention to the lowly, the hurt and the ailing, the exiled and the scorned of His time. In 20 years of work among poor people here and abroad, I have found Christ's life a constant source of inspiration to this century's poor. They attend His words. They regard closely His manner of living. They do not overlook the company He kept, those ordinary working people who would have been unremarked by history were it not for Him. Nor is such attentiveness to God on the part of people sorely in need to be regarded as a kind of hypnotic diversion, an anodyne for the desperate masses among whom ignorance and superstitiousness are rife. When one presses the above-quoted lady on the matter of poverty (hers and that of everyone around her), one obtains an exceedingly shrewd appraisal of what fate offers and why: "I do not think God wanted everyone to be poor! I don't think He said to Himself, let there be a lot of people in Rio who can't get enough to eat, and a few, a very few, who are covered with gold and diamonds, and worry only that they shouldn't get too fat for their 1,000 dresses or 1,000 suits! I think God knew that only He could bring goodness to the earth—only He could make people as kind to each other as He was to everyone. But that happens in the world He rules! He doesn't rule this world! He is not to be found running the Copacabana! He didn't rule the world He visited when He came to us a long time ago.

"I am sure God would like us all to be rich, but He isn't the one to stay around, every day, giving us miracles! He came here, and that was a miracle, and He told us if we wanted to see Him again, we should remember His words, and we should never forget how He lived. That is what our nuns tell us, and that is the truth. I only hope and pray that if someone discovered a diamond mine under my house, and I became the richest person in all of Brazil, I'd remember what I just said!"

She comprehended, out of the depths of her suffering life, the existential paradoxes Christ posed to all of us—that one can have a lot, yet be utterly lacking, and that one can be in the greatest of jeopardy, and thereby be more likely by virtue of one's predicament to take keen notice of the very urgent messages sent the world by Isaiah and Jeremiah and Amos, by Jesus Christ and His disciples. That woman trembled in a humble appreciation of this life's mysteries and ironies; and so have others the world over. Many of us, unfortunately, have no interest in acknowledging the significance the Bible's revelations have for the poor, the uneducated, the dispossessed—all those who make up the overwhelming majority of so many nations. Bread is what she and her family need, we correctly insist; and education and more economic opportunity and increased political leverage and on and on. She would be the last one to deny such a claim. She is not opiated with resignation, indifferent to the things of this world. She is simply willing to take a look at the world in this manner: "I look at Christ every day—over there, across the city, on the hill. I think of how hard His life was. He was crucified, even if He was God. No, He was crucified *because* He was God. Oh, I can't figure out why He was crucified! I can't figure out why I was born so poor. But I do know this: Jesus is someone for all of us. He lives in my heart. But those who killed Him did so a long time ago, and no one knows them. It's best to remember that, and I do. He loved us, the poor, and He lives. The big shots who ran the country where He lived cared nothing about Him, or us, and they disappeared. I tell my children: that is lesson number one for them to learn, and never, never forget, however long they live."

April 1982

Christ and the Rich

For a number of years I worked with children who belonged to quite comfortable, if not wealthy, families. I did so in the South during the 1960s, and later, in the North. I wanted to know how white and black children caught in our nation's recent racial struggles managed; but I also wanted to know how other children, quite removed from the strain of social change, regarded the events taking place in the lives of their fellow American age-mates. As I went about talking with the various protagonists who confronted each other in cities such as New Orleans and Atlanta, or Boston and Cleveland, I soon enough met prominent lawyers or businessmen, or newspaper publishers or bankers, who lived at a great remove from the particular strife plaguing the cities where their offices were located—and who worried long and hard about what would happen, given the seemingly ineradicable fear, suspicion, and hate that plagued the particular metropolitan region in question. It was the children of such individuals whom I got to know fairly well.

One such well-to-do man, a lawyer born to an extremely prominent Louisiana family, put the torment New Orleans was experiencing during 1960 and 1961 in the following perspective: "There's always been trouble between people—between nations and races, between the rich and the poor. I remember my ancient history, and my modern European history, and my American history! I remember the Bible, too—all the conflict you read about in the Old Testament, and even when God became a Man, yes, even with Jesus among us, the conflict didn't go away. So, I tell my children that they have to keep in mind what people are like—how bad we all can be at certain moments. Sometimes, though, we'll come back from church and one of my kids will start asking me those questions—those whys that make you want to run out of the house and play golf, or go for a long ride, *alone,* in your car! And when the Bible gets into the act—your son or daughter quoting Jesus to you!—then it really is time to flee for your life!"

That last remark, stated so casually, if not impulsively, may have been one of the most biblical moments I will ever experience—the sight and sound of a professing Christian aware that he was in deep spiritual trouble! Moments later he would remind me of Christ's life—tell me, really, that he, a rich and powerful 20th-century American, knew full well the particular burden *he* carried, never mind that borne by the poor, the black, the socially or occupationally marginal: "I was taken to church from my earliest days. My uncle is an Episcopalian minister. I know the Old Testament and the New Testament! I can find passages to justify segregation, and to make me feel good about this life I've always enjoyed, and always will enjoy, until I die. But I have a legal mind, and I majored in English—liked literary criticism, textual analysis—and so I can't overlook what I read. I can't turn a clear-cut message into a confusing one. Jesus told us that the Devil has many disguises, one of them Mammon! He gave us that unforgettable image of the camel trying to get through the eye of a needle. Well, I guess I'm one big camel, and even now, I can anticipate the crunch I'll be in! I don't mean this humor to be offensive; it's the kind of humor Dante must have had in mind when he called his work *The Divine Comedy!*"

A moment or two in a long life! He is now over 60, and still wrestling with such matters, I can report—still wrestling, I think he'd want me to say, with the Devil, as do we all, rich or poor or in between. He knows in his bones that there is indeed an incongruity between Christ's chosen life, as we are reminded of it in Scripture, and the lives of so many of us live today—so secure, easy, protected, if not downright extravagant and endlessly self-enhancing. Maybe such a lack of symmetry is one of history's tricks, fate's accidents. Maybe we were not all meant to follow Him, over the centuries, as did His disciples—their radical surrender to His impoverished, vulnerable, and ultimately fatal destiny. Short of Heaven and Hell, no one can claim to know for sure what His will, finally, was meant to be, so far as we of this and other centuries to come are concerned. And yet—one adds that qualifying phrase immediately, and with some apprehension: and yet, the life of Jesus Christ was not meant to go unnoticed by those of us who address Him with devotion in church and at home. How far ought we follow His example? Shall we try to follow His lead, for instance, at work—as we engage ourselves with others, who are "below" us in station, in position, in rank, or class? Shall we, day in and day out, try to take heed of His advice—that all eternity hangs on the manner of life we pursue, one of humility and generosity and compassion, or one of self-importance, self-cultivation, and eager pursuit of this world's various blandishments?

Such questions are impossible ones, in a way, to answer in any quick or categorical manner. The Christ who brought us "not peace but a sword" had scant interest, one suspects, in our "peace of mind," or our "mental equilibrium." He lived a life provocative in the extreme. He was a scandal to church and empire alike. He died a declared outcast, lowly thieves at His side. No matter the splendor of our churches, no matter the money and power wielded in His name, or offered up as gifts to His memory, His example is hard to forget—the way He chose to spend His time among us, not to mention the company He kept. My New Orleans friend, I suspect, was right to think of Him as the migrant who crossed Galilee, ever keeping company with those born in the wrong place, those down on their luck, those hurt and ailing; and my friend was also right to think of himself, so rich in today's America, as in jeopardy *sub specie aeternitatis,* no matter the size and diversification of his stock portfolio.

May 1982

Christ and the Intellectuals

For many years, as I have worked in various parts of this country, trying to understand how all sorts of families make do, often against considerable odds, I have sent periodic reports to interested fellow citizens—the articles and books of a particular writer. Soon enough, I have received the expected responses: comments from colleagues and friends; letters from readers; and not least, reviews or essays mentioning my work, among that of others. After awhile I began to learn a lot about my prejudices and blind-spots, as one only does, perhaps, through the eyes of others. However, I think I also began to learn about the prevailing assumptions of others, my fellow writers and critics.

Especially revealing were the issues in my work I saw scrutinized by others. When I was not enough the social scientist, they took quick notice. When I was too much so—willing to dish out a clever and glib or facile generalization—they also took notice. When I was unconsciously wordy they quite properly took issue; and when I was presumptuously terse or indirect, they also let me know. The toughest critics were, in a way, the best to read: one's pride hurt, but one's head shaken loose of a few barnacles. One critic got to the heart of a certain overwrought, fuzzy loquacity which, I regret to say, has informed some of my writing—and, too, a gushy sentimentality that has, on occasion, seemed irrepressibly indiscreet.

I say all this not in an orgy of masochism, but to indicate that mix of resentment and gratitude I suspect many of my ilk feel toward their own ilk—the "intelligentsia" or the "intellectual community," to use the dreary, self-important expressions. On one score, though, I confess to perplexity, even alarm—an absence, almost total, of reaction, never mind criticism, when it has come to an entire side of my work, and the writing that I've done with respect to it. I refer to

22

the descriptions I've rendered of the religious thoughts and feelings of the children and adults I've come to know.

All I need do, it seems, is come up with a social conclusion, make a psychological generalization, attempt a literary analysis, try portraying a certain kind of personal or community or regional life, and there are thoughtful (appreciatively or reprovingly so) correspondents or essayists willing to share their evaluations with others publicly. But when I have tried to describe how, say, an old Spanish-speaking woman of the northern part of New Mexico, or a Southern black child, or an Appalachian white child, or a suburban housewife, or a small-town working-class man happen to feel about God and His life and words and deeds, then the result is either the silence already mentioned, or rarely, a puzzled, frustrated truculence: "I don't see why you get yourself into all that religious talk! It just goes on and on! If you're trying to prove that people are superstitious, or need a crutch, then a page is enough, not a chapter or a half of a book!" Part of a letter from a friend—a college teacher, no less; and someone anxious as can be to know about this or that person's political "orientation" or social standing or cultural point of view.

In my own case, often enough, the attention given religious faith is held even more suspect, if not bizarre, because I'm a psychiatrist—and so, presumably, "educated" and "perceptive" enough (so I was told in another friendly letter!) to "know better"! I should be what an intellectual ought be—someone who analyzes how others think and feel, who gives reasons for one or another social crisis or moment of history. The civil rights struggle, for instance: I ought have kept my mind on the various "variables," domestic and foreign, that prompted it—the why, when, and where of the matter. What matters to so many of us contemporary intellectuals is *explanations*—for example, a discussion of the "motivations" of the activists who fought segregation in the 1960s. To what class did they belong? What were their "relevant" childhood experiences? Meanwhile, there is this young man, from Birmingham, Alabama, speaking in 1965: "I don't know why I put myself on the line. I don't know why I said no to segregation. I'm just another white Southerner, and I wasn't brought up to love integration! But I was brought up to love Jesus Christ, and when I saw the police of this city use dogs on people, I asked myself what Jesus Christ would have thought, and what He would have done—and that's all I know about how I came to be here, on the firing line!"

I probed and pushed, and got no further with him. I very much wanted to get further, wanted explanations I considered "deeper," more (and again the word) "relevant." So with blacks, too—those men and women and children who were so urgently, so professedly Christian: the Very Reverend Martin Luther King, the Very Reverend Fred Shuttlesworth, the Very Reverend Andrew Young. I talked with them and their followers, and even though I heard them in churches all over the South praying hard, crying loud, acknowledging His inspiration and calling for His succor, I was deaf to all that—interested, as I thought I must be, in social traumas and emotional hurdles and racial inequities, all of which, needless to say, certainly deserved documentation. But we also have to document what people believe, and how their beliefs prompt them to live their lives. And I fear that when I started doing that, rather earnestly, I learned something about myself and my kind—how arrogant and self-centered we risk becoming: interested in our own heady assertions, and anxious to be the spokespersons for all those others, who don't write and teach and come up with new and significant ideas, but who, rather, try to go from one day to the next, and who yes, in large numbers indeed, keep calling on Jesus Christ, not the intellectuals, for guidance.

June 1982

Spiritual Kinship

On certain days a letter will come, a student's paper will arrive, an article or book will command my attention—and I end up saying to myself about the particular writer: he or she is spiritual kin. Similarly with a person in the flesh—one talks for a while, and certain shared values and assumptions prompt a sense of companionship that I prefer to think of as not only psychological or intellectual, but grounded in extremely important and mutually held ideals (not to be confused with ideas). I sense that something spiritual is taking place, for example, when a Harvard student, bright as can be and able to rise to the top of a significantly capable scholarly community, points out to me with an aroused conviction the following quotation from *The Imitation of Christ:* "Deeply inquisitive reasoning does not make a man holy or righteous but a good life makes him beloved by God. I would rather feel compunction of heart for my sins than merely know the definition of compunction." And further along, the "admonitions" Thomas à Kempis offered posterity: "The more knowledge you have, the more grievously will you be judged for its misuse, if you do not live according to it."

The issue is not, of course, whether one agrees or disagrees with such remarks. They can be regarded, by skeptics, as banal and unexceptional; as rhetorical, and of little moral significance in the day-to-day world of practical and competitive challenge; or, as yet additional instances of an anti-intellectual tradition. But the student in question was not being sloppy or smug or pompous; nor had he any strong interest in denigrating his own intelligence, or that of others around him. He was keenly interested, however, in St. Paul's well-known distinction between the letter and the spirit, and he saw in a 15th-century monk's writing a resonance with St. Paul, even as he saw a similar resonance in the writings of Walker Percy, who makes mention of a person who (I love to quote this whenever an opportunity presents itself) "got all A's, and flunked life."

That same student was not unwilling to dip into the secular tradition for comparisons. He points out to me that when Ralph Waldo Emerson asserted to his mid-19th century Cambridge, Massachusetts, listeners a certain hierarchy of things—namely, "character is higher than intellect"—he was mindful of the same question Thomas à Kempis considered: the uses to which we put this or that well-muscled factuality. Of course, for Emerson, Nature was all, an outlook my young friend finds austere, if not bleak. Still, his generosity of spirit (*not* to be confused with ecumenicism, which can often enough turn into an abdication of religious principles or faith itself) was prompting a desire to find common ideals in people of various (even contrary) convictions.

That central issue of abstract study preoccupies a number of writers and readers, and I think there *is* a spiritual kinship among those who are alarmed, even frightened, by a kind of scholarly life that goes full steam ahead, year after year, with no self-criticism, no moral anxiety, no sense of mocking humor with respect to itself. Emerson may have been as near to Christianity with the above-quoted comment as he would ever get (and the possibility of a terrible arrogance, if not sinfulness, being part of that immediately preceding observation ought be put on the record). I mean this: once the intellect casts suspicion on its solo exertions, a kind of religious inquiry has begun: we are asking Who or What prompts such a gesture of humility—such an act of renunciation? I think those of us who have experienced our own grievous pride, and tried falling on our knees symbolically (maybe even literally!) are experts at noticing a similar act of contrition (oh, these days we have to settle for a variant of self-analysis!) in others. There is an important connection made—and it has to do with the moral or existential life, hence the word "spiritual."

Another very fine young friend of mine, a Duke University student, also evoked that expression "spiritual kinship" in my mind recently when he wrote a paper full of references to his tearfulness—his sadness in the face of the hurt he sees everywhere. Many of us experience our painful recognition of suffering, needless to say. But this young man was going a step further; he was asking why there is so much meanness in this world, and what *he* ought to do to make a difference in that regard, and not least, under the sanction of which philosophical or religious set of beliefs. Put differently, he was making the world's pain his own—rather than distancing it as a fit subject for "analysis." He was thinking (out of a childhood in a minister's home) in the Christian tradition—which is exceptionally demanding personally, because it differs from all other religions in just this respect: Christ become man, hence consenting to take upon Himself voluntarily what others must willy-nilly bear. I felt in that wonderfully thoughtful student the presence of not just an admirable psychological "trait" (the stuff of this age's mental exertions) but a quality of grace I found inspiring, a quality toward which I hoped to aspire myself, hence the notion of "spiritual kinship" in my head as we talked, and later, corresponded.

One final instance—this drawn from the writing of Simone Weil: "Culture is a privilege that gives power to the class that possesses it ... [and so] let us try to undermine this privilege by relating complicated knowledge to the commonest knowledge." She was telling us that in this godless time, those who conjure up abstractions obtain adulation if not a posture of idolatrous submission from others, more desperate for some faith, any faith, than they may realize. She was being, of course, self-critical. But she was also asking her readers—ironically apt to bow to her—that they regard closely their own possibilities, or more sadly, fatal inclinations. Such a passage in a writer's book can become for a reader something more than edifying; can become a moment of companionship—the spiritual kinship that Christ offered us as He walked Galilee, and the same spiritual kinship to which we in later centuries try to connect ourselves, now and then, through each other's commitments of heart and soul.

July–August 1982

Simone Weil's Faith

I well remember a seminar of Paul Tillich's during the mid-1950s when the subject of Simone Weil surfaced. Immediately, her death came into question (she died in August 1943). She lived to be 34, and was, someone asserted, responsible for the brief duration of her life because she was "sick"—not just with tuberculosis, but in her head. She was "anorectic," someone else said. Yet another authoritative voice pronounced her "psychotic." She had terrible migraine headaches, we were reminded, and everyone in the 20th century knows what causes *them!*

When psychology was finally laid to rest, we began with politics. Simone Weil was a fatuous anarchist of sorts. True, she opposed capitalism and Communism both, and true, she wanted the poor to live better, much better. But she had no specific allegiance to a party, a program, a means of implementing a more egalitarian society. A demurrer that *The Need for Roots,* published posthumously, contained a wide-ranging series of proposals, was dismissed out-of-hand on the grounds of the "speculative" and "impractical" nature of her social essays. And, indeed, the French resistance leaders (including General de Gaulle) who read her proposals for the post-war world felt she was, to put it mildly, utopian.

I remember my annoyance with the members of that seminar— and not least, with myself (I kept my mouth shut). I remember my disappointment, too, with Tillich—his unwillingness, at least on that occasion, to take Simone Weil's serious challenges both to 20th-century Communism and contemporary Christianity as seriously as I thought their due. I had read her *Gravity and Grace,* been touched enormously by her commanding, sparkling literary and philosophical sensibility—tamed valiantly out of respect to the mystery of God and His Son. Shortly thereafter I ventured further, read her *Notebooks,* read her *Oppression and Liberty,* read her various essays and letters collected under several titles both here and in Europe (e.g., *Seventy Letters, Selected Essays*). Eventually a long biography by her friend Simone Pétrement *(Simone Weil: A Life)* would give us detailed information about this extraordinary pilgrim's life.

She was born to an agnostic, well-to-do, Parisian Jewish family in 1909. Her father was a physician. Her brother André would one day be a distinguished mathematician at the Princeton Institute for Advanced Studies. As a young child she worried about the poor, the needy. She also was, early on, a brilliant author. She and Simone de Beauvoir were contenders, of sorts, in school—each enormously erudite and able to win over others through written (and, one gathers, oral) argument.

Yet, this exceptionally promising intellectual rather quickly turned her back on the conventional academic life; she preferred to teach in a secondary school—and soon enough, to learn how ordinary working people manage to make do under the constraints of, say, a particular factory or a farm. She tried working on assembly lines or harvesting crops, not in a self-indulgent romanticism or slumming—a prelude, perhaps, to yet another account of how "they" get along. She saw injustice, of course, and wanted to challenge it, but only from within, so to speak. She knew she was not poor; nor was she ever ready to live an utterly impoverished life. But she also knew that Christ's suffering life, so clearly connected by Him to that of other sufferers—the poor, the ailing, the "rebuked and scorned"—was an example of sorts. She refused the bourgeois affirmations and consolations available to herself, while all the time learning of the indignity so many others had to take for granted.

She was a loner, an unyielding partisan in a moral conflict the dimensions of which, maybe, only she comprehended. She was passionately in love with God, with Jesus, as one comes to realize upon reading *Gravity and Grace.* She read and reread and reread George Herbert's poem "Love." She saw the Cross as *the* central element in Christianity—the great, demanding presence, still, in our lives, if we would only know it: God's embrace of our vulnerability, and yes, God's victory over pride. She struggled to the end with her own pride—that of a talented intellectual. She aimed for a kind of triumph over the self—and so trying, she may well have sinned grievously, because there is a kind of pride that expresses itself in a feverish assault on pride (an ironic, amplified, self-denunciating pride).

Simone Weil is often called a secular saint, but she would bristle at such a designation, and mock those who use it. She refused entrance to the Catholic Church because she wanted to be with hurt and sad outsiders at all costs. The Church was the property of too many contented, self-important burghers, she felt. She was a primitive Christian, I suppose—very much, one suspects, like those women who revered Christ, yearned to attend Him. She didn't starve herself to death; nor was she crazy. She kept her food intake at the level of that available to the people of German-occupied France. Her own family had escaped, with her, to America, where (in New York City) she quickly found herself at home in the black fundamentalist churches of Harlem. She had rather soon, however, left for England, where, during the London blitz, she worked for the Free French forces. She wanted to be flown to France, to work in the underground resistance. She wanted to help build a world in which Christ's teachings were law—not easily mouthed pieties, but burned into the hearts of everyone.

She was a dreamer, an impossible idealist; and it can even be argued she was a heretic, all too hard on the flesh, and rather wrongly anxious to separate the spirit of Christ from His concrete and particular existence. Still, she labored hard in the vineyard of Faith, eagerly in pursuit of the Jesus Who walked Galilee, preaching and healing, reaching out all the time to those in need, in duress, in one or another kind of exile. No wonder we, in a high and mighty university during the "quiet" 1950s (and no matter, it seemed, the religious nature of the course we took), found this utterly passionate soul, so given to a pursuit of Jesus Christ, to be a thoroughly incomprehensible figure. The haunting question, always, is whether Christ Himself would fare any better in our minds, at least with many of us, were He to appear in one or another presence among us.

September 1982

Bonhoeffer's Courage—
and Our Lives

I teach (with Robert Kiely) a course for Harvard undergraduates titled "The Literature of Christian Reflection." We start with Augustine and Pascal and end with Dietrich Bonhoeffer. I give the lecture on Bonhoeffer, and each spring struggle with his writings, with the massive biography of him by his dear friend Eberhard Bethge, and not least, with his astonishing (and exemplary) life. Each year that life is the source of speculation, even as the book *Letters and Papers from Prison* both stirs and frightens the students, not to mention their teachers. One decent and contemplative youth, a senior from a strongly Lutheran Minnesota family, wrote the following words as part of an essay on Bonhoeffer: "It is a terrible decision—to take up arms against your own government. And even more unusual to do so when you know death is likely."

Here is a student of our 1980s America who quite eagerly acknowledges the obedience he feels toward a nation, and who enjoys life enough to find the prospect of an early chosen death almost unthinkable. Moreover, he pointed out what is so important about Bonhoeffer's fate—that it was quite avoidable, had he turned from the particular course he had set for himself. Bonhoeffer's heroism was that of the lucky, well-to-do person who has no reason to fear exclusion as a result of his race, religion, or social position. He was born (in 1906) to a distinguished German family; his father was a psychiatrist who taught at the University of Berlin. His relatives and ancestors were clergymen, lawyers, political leaders, and high-standing soldiers. By 1924 he had decided to pursue a degree in theology. In 1928 he left Germany to serve as a pastor to a church in Barcelona, Spain. In 1930 he came to America for a stretch of studies at Union Theological Seminary. He returned to Berlin in 1931 to teach theology, but with the advent of Nazism his days in both the classroom and pulpit were numbered. By 1936 he was already under surveillance for his clear opposition to Hitler. In that regard, *The Cost of Discipleship* (1937) was extremely important, and to this day—in all cultures and situations—that book connects with the very heart of the Christian life: how much of one's everyday comfort is one willing to surrender in pursuit of His (as opposed to our) imperatives?

Bonhoeffer derided "cheap grace" in that book, and elsewhere. He did not understand how believing Christians could expect to eat of this day's self-enhancement, indifference, craven greed, meanness, and hatefulness, all the while expecting and preparing themselves (as Sunday communicants, say) for the cake of God's favorable recognition. What is more, he proceeded in a quiet yet determined manner to live out his ideas. Put differently, he had no interest in moral analysis or moral rhetoric unconnected to the possibilities and predicaments of a given life. He seemed intent on really testing his own ideas: how persuasive were they with respect to *his* actions—never mind those of others? He worried, I suppose it can be said, about the "cheap grace" afforded intellectuals, self-appointed moralists, preachers, ideologues of various persuasions— who tell others what is good and bad, what and what not to do, and yet manage to escape the pain or sacrifice entailed in all sorts of ethically demanding trials.

In 1939, as war threatened, he was in America on a speaking tour. He was urged to remain. A return to Hitler's Germany meant terrible risks, even death. But he did not hesitate; he took one of the last ships to leave for Germany before the onset of the blitzkrieg into Poland. From then on it was only a matter of time before he would be arrested. He worked on his *Ethics,* which (though incomplete) was published posthumously in 1949. But he also worked in the German resistance—an effort on the part of decent and honorable people to overthrow Hitler, which reached its tragic moments of crisis on July 20, 1944, when a carefully planned assassination attempt on *Der Führer* failed. Even before that sad day, Bonhoeffer had been spotted for the man he, indeed, was—a brave political antagonist of extremely powerful "principalities and powers," a pastor almost single-handedly taking on a nation then in control of virtually all Europe. In early April of 1943 he was arrested, and in April of 1945, now at notorious Buchenwald, he was killed by the Gestapo. His last known words, spoken to a fellow inmate, were these: "This is the end—for me the beginning of life."

One offers the above biographical information in no mere narrative exercise. Here was a life that transcended a brilliant mind's achievements; a life that makes biographical presentation the utter "heart of the matter," to use that phrase in the spiritual sense Graham Greene did; a life that still poses a strong challenge at any and every passing reader: what really counts in this life morally? Rather obviously, each of us has his or her particular span of time to experience—bound always by the accidents of circumstance. Bonhoeffer's idealistic nature, his reverential Christianity, and his alert, activist conscience had to confront an awful historical moment—which, nevertheless, proved ironically to be for certain individuals an instrument of grace. Hellish times (such are the paradoxes of this earthly existence) can pave the way to heaven for some. But not by any means for all: Germany was full of supposedly good and decent people—not a few talking or writing a big ethical line—who were only too willing to sign up with Hitler's henchmen. Still others kept a discreet silence—and lived.

What makes for courage—for the man or woman who is ready, in a time of danger, to take the greatest possible chances on behalf of his or her faith? I doubt anyone has a specific answer to such a question. To ask it is, one hopes and prays, a beginning for each of us—a kind of prayer that if and when a trial should come upon us, we would be ready and waiting. But one can never know—whether one would do honor in the field of action to one's principles, or even when that moment of testing will, in fact, arrive. Hitler was a special kind of anti-Christ. In all our lives there are comparatively lesser devils to confront—but they are no less significant, one suspects, in their capacity to reveal the truth of ourselves. Such is what Jesus knew as He walked Galilee, reminding His people that in the smallest ways, in the least dramatic moments, our character can emerge.

As for the "mind," where these days so much is supposed to take place, I have seen little in what we call "psychology" or "psychiatry" to be of much help, when it comes to figuring out who will do what, and when. People of my kind spend a lot of time trying to comprehend how things have gone sour for the people we see in our offices. We haven't even begun to understand the mystery of goodness; of lovingkindness become the dominant attribute of a life; of bravery exerted on behalf of decent persuasion; of life itself yielded not in despair or out of "masochism" or "narcissistic grandiosity," but in simple, humble acquiescence to virtuous conviction. And Lord, when the day comes that we even start being interested in such matters, we may ourselves stand a better chance of measuring up to—well, to His example, lived for us 2,000 years ago.

October 1982

Who Is to Be Pitied?

The poor, sad, old lady, her world circumscribed, her education so limited, her prospects so grim—this is what I thought as I was first getting to know her in the summer of 1972. She lived in Truchas, New Mexico, a small town amid the Sangre de Cristo Mountains, well north of Santa Fe's cultural cosmopolitan life. She is of a people often characterized as Hispano-Americans—here for generations before "Anglos" (as she calls quite another kind of American) even deigned to settle in North America. All her life, all the life of her husband, all the lives of her four sons and three daughters (and their husbands) have been given over to hard farm work, to cutting and selling wood, to occasional odd jobs in a community essentially still pastoral in nature. All her life, too, has been given to the local Catholic Church.

I got to know her because she was the grandmother of one of the children I had met while working in a nearby school. I was trying to find out how children in a particular part of America grew up—in contrast to the children from more familiar (middle-class, suburban, Anglo) circumstances, whom I knew as the person I am (a parent, a physician). All I could do was comment (in the notes I was keeping) on the handicaps, the flaws, the deficits, the "problems"— which, in sum, amounted to the unpromising heritage of a people left in the lurch, it seems, while the rest of us have done so very well. But the wrinkled, wry, slightly stooped, composed Mrs. Santander begged again and again to differ with me. During one week I sat with her three times, and heard the thrust of her argument take various shapes—as in this pointed assertion: "You have so much pity in your eyes, you have yet to see us. All you see is *your* pity given *our* flesh!"

Such shrewd, jarring flashes of wisdom can, of course, be readily

35

dismissed by a 20th-century American social scientist, all too sure of his intellectual prerogatives, and adept at the use of psychology as a polemical and self-serving weapon: alas, yet another "defensive," frightened "informant," striking a blow at a visitor out of not only insecurity but a sense of futility, of worthlessness. There were, however, further such statements; their cumulative weight was, please God, rather astonishing to my family, as we all got to hear a lady just under 85 say a few things about herself, her life—and ourselves, our lives: "I was walking with our dog; she is 10, and has not much more time with us. As we move, I think of God; I am sure He will soon call both of us! Suddenly, that afternoon, a beautiful silence was broken. The sky exploded. The trees trembled. Our village stopped in its tracks. My dog stopped, then she got down on her hind legs, and started crying—a low, soft noise. I got down on my legs, too; I took my Rosary in my hands, and started praying. All I could see was our Lord on the Cross, and the Virgin Mary, her eyes full of tears, wishing the world was a better world, so her Son would not have to die.

"A moment later 'they' were gone—two of the Anglo planes. My son says those planes are the fastest we have. My son says they can go faster than the speed noise travels, and they can carry those bombs that make an exploding volcano seem like one of my grandchildren's firecrackers. I watched them go, and then I got up and I tried to talk with God. I said something like this to Him: 'Oh, dear Lord, when will You lose patience with those Anglos? Look what they are doing, right here in New Mexico.' The Anglo teachers tell my grandchildren, in school, that they are in lots of trouble: they don't speak right, and they don't think like people do in Santa Fe and Albuquerque. They're not Anglos! They are only themselves—little people, without money, and no big education. Some of our Spanish-speaking people say we should get 'power.' I heard them in Truchas right in front of the Church, the other day. Oh, yes: power! The Devil's power, if you ask me! Think of those planes, those bombs, the dirt in the air, the poison in the water, the crookedness all over! I hear the Anglos talking about themselves on our radio—what they plan to do to our land. They grab it, they take anything they can find in it, they leave it. They have hidden in our mountains bombs that can wipe out all life. They have ruined our rivers. They sink their wells deeper and deeper in our hills. They rush in here from all over—and soon they will be gone. While they're here, they round up Indians, and treat us like stupid slaves.

"When I think about such things, I want to pray for my family, for my people. I want God to come and help us. I want Him to get angry, as He did in Jerusalem, just before He was taken and killed. But our priest reminds us that in the end Jesus was not angry; He was forgiving. So, I try to forgive! I stop praying for my own family, for my neighbors; I pray, instead, for all of the Anglos in Albuquerque—the ones I've heard my children and grandchildren describe, the ones I sometimes see driving through here, throwing out their garbage, stirring up the dust with their cars, honking their horns if (God forbid!) my goats get in their way. No one should get in their way! Not even God's commandments; not even His words, or the words of His good friends, kept for us in the Bible.

"If I only could pray longer and harder for the Anglos! I give up a lot. I find myself crying for them, but suddenly my face turns to fire. I want to scream. Then I think of Jesus, and am ashamed of myself, and down on my knees again, trying to behave like one of His children, and knowing I'll be lucky, as one of my grandchildren says, if I'll 'get a C' from Him!"

She has her blind-spots and personal weaknesses. She is not going to give us a solution to our many and vexing national problems. But there is in her, one eventually begins to recognize, a complex, thoughtful, deeply reverential (and, of course, pastoral) Christian vision of how this world ought to be—how we should get along with each other. Her pity often gave way to bitterness; she was a human being. But the objects of her pity (my ilk, I fear) are not known, all the time, for their boundless compassion. Nor is Jesus Christ, for so many of us ever so well-educated and successful Anglos, the living presence He was for her all her long life—right unto her death in 1975.

November 1982

Belfast's Christian Tribes

For seven years now I have been visiting particular neighborhoods in Belfast—Northern Ireland's great port city. I've wanted to learn how children acquire a set of loyalties—or fail to do so. I've wanted to understand the way children become, in their own minds, *Irish,* or *Protestant,* or *Catholic,* or *Anglican,* or citizens of the *British Isles,* or whatever: connected to a faith, a nationality, a moral point of view, a geographic entity. When in childhood do such connections take place, with what degree of conviction, and to what effect?

I am no stranger to this kind of work. I started talking with children about their lives (as opposed to their problems) when I was training to be a child psychiatrist at the Children's Hospital in Boston. At one time (the mid-1950s) polio was still a dreaded disease; vaccines, bearing their mercy, would come a few years later. I found myself talking with boys and girls who, suddenly, were paralyzed. Their "problems" were connected, not to family conflict or unconscious "processes," but rather to those old variables that Job and St. Paul knew so well: fate, chance, circumstance, accident. How hard we try, today, to banish such aspects of life, sweep them under one or another cover, called a theory, an ideology, an explanation, all meant to conceal from us our naked vulnerability in the face of that larger scheme of things: mysteries such as time, space, and matter—not to mention God's will and presence. I doubt I'll ever forget what one lad—10 years old, and after three days of fever and muscle aches paralyzed from the waist down—said to me: "The doctors try to tell me why, but no one knows why. They say it's a virus, but then they say the virus is everywhere, and I ask them why I'm the one who can't move my legs, and the doctors stop talking. Like my favorite teacher says: 'It's best sometimes to admit you

don't know, and then shut up.' If you know *something* . . . there's
[also] a lot you don't know, and a lot you'll never know, and that's
not so bad, because at least you don't get a big head." *A big head!*
The sin of pride, the besetting sin of so many of us who teach and
write, who preach or offer psychological interpretations, who make
it our business to tell others what to think and how to live their
lives.

And now, a quarter of a century later, I find myself talking with
other children and with their parents, who live in another part of
the world, and who struggle with another kind of paralysis—and
who try, as that child quoted above tried, to make sense of this life's
riddles and occasional spells of craziness. Here is a 12-year-old
Catholic child of Belfast's Ardoyne district trying to comprehend
this vexing world: "My grannie says I should think of Jesus Christ
every day, at least once. I tell her I do; I tell her there will be a day
when I think of Him 10 times in 10 minutes! I think of Him
especially when the bombs go off, and when the Brits come at us
with their sticks and their hoses and their guns. I think of him when
the IRA knocks one of the Brits off; or when one of ours gets killed
for being 'friendly' with the Brits. 'It's all religion, our troubles
here,' my grampa said, and I thought of Jesus then, and saw my
grannie sewing, and I asked her if *she* was thinking of Jesus, then
and there, like I was, and she said, 'Lord, no!' I was set to ask her
why, but I think she knew what I had on the tip of my tongue,
because she told me to 'shoo,' and I did, real fast. She slipped me a
sweet as I ran off!"

Lots to interpret in that working-class parlor scene! Most of all,
there was the child's awareness of a given incongruity: a so-called
religious struggle being waged with passionate hate, murderous
vengeance. Of course, Ulster's "troubles" are also social, political,
and economic: the Protestants are by and large privileged; the
Catholics are often enough hard-pressed, confined to menial work,
or jobless in all too significant numbers. Still, the rhetoric is religious. Christ is every day summoned on behalf of the Catholic
Ardoyne, or, as the following words of a 12-year-old girl illustrate,
on behalf of the Protestant Shankill neighborhood: "We have to
watch out for the Papists; they are out to rule everyone. They have
a dozen children to the family. They don't worship Jesus; they
worship the pope. They are bad, and if they would only leave and
go live in Dublin, we'd have peace here. The day will come when

Jesus Christ will get tired of them; I know that. Our minister says they are the anti-Christ, and my mom says it means they're against Christ, and He'll give them a proper licking one day!"

I asked (in provocative ignorance and innocence, I fear) what she meant when she spoke of a "proper licking." She replied, "Oh, he'll take them all on His knees and hit them hard, and then He'll send them away for good." I was troubled by this prophecy of radical estrangement, so far as thousands and thousands of professing Christians are concerned.

All in all, I've seen Belfast's people assemble themselves as militant Christian tribalists, a sad spectacle, indeed. On both sides one hears evidence of the old arrogance and smugness and self-importance which go, collectively, with any sort of tribalism. I cringe and get angry when I hear social scientists or my psychiatric colleagues do so—strut about, proclaiming *their* (exclusive, utterly unique) truths, not rarely expressed in the dreariest, most disedifying language. I also cringe and get angry when I hear loud-mouthed politicians do likewise. But it is truly painful (a stab in one's moral and spiritual heart) to be reminded that throughout history our Lord Jesus Christ has been calumnied, used, and abused, by those who claim Him defiantly, possessively, polemically, those who deny Him to others, and even make war and kill in His name. Our Lord is, as Dorothy Day put it, "the suffering Christ whom professed Christians betray, day after day."

December 1982

Georges Bernanos and
the Catholic Church

In my teaching, a grave moment comes each year, the week when I must lecture on Georges Bernanos, on his novels *The Diary of a Country Priest* and *Mouchette,* and on his complicated and unusual religious journey. I find that the great majority of students have never heard of him or his stories, his anguished spiritual essays, his wonderfully passionate and sometimes choleric political journalism. Even the great French film maker Robert Bresson (a good friend of Bernanos) fails, often enough, to win the students over to Bernanos with his version of *The Diary of a Country Priest.* "Too slow," I hear rather frequently from young men and women who have found a certain tricky celluloid speed to be the *sine qua non* of a satisfying two hours in the magic dark of a theater.

Sometimes, however, *The Diary* does indeed "take"; and then the affected student becomes hungry for more information about a particular, idiosyncratic Christian pilgrim: "I've never read a book like that one. The priest haunts me. I see my own life as I read about his—the vanity and the blundering pride I try to spot in others, so I won't see them in myself! Also, the struggle with commitment to an institution: The Catholic Church is a means of Grace, but it's also full of people who are fallible and ridiculous, and sometimes downright malicious, as all of us are, if not one day, then another!"

The more indifferent students are right, though: Bernanos and his young curé—struggling in the midst of an obscure, rain-drenched French rural community to make sure of his religious vocation, of his Church's claims, and to figure out our nature as finite creatures obsessed, nevertheless, with matters of infinite importance—are hardly a duo for lots of today's swinging, "with it"

41

Americans. The curé, God save him, has doubts, catches himself being self-important and thoughtless of the difficulties experienced by others. The curé notices that his preaching to others serves, upon occasion, the great convenience of letting himself go scot-free morally. The curé works hard to be a quiet, reflective, kindly person who ministers to others, and obtains satisfaction in *their* moments of virtue. The curé is a man who, finally, has no great faith in the intellect, in psychological awareness, in sweeping political change, in this or that evidence of "progress." He sees, everywhere, not only the possibility of grace, but that sin of sins, pride, in its countless, coy disguises. Relentlessly, *The Diary* offers us readers a glimpse at smug intellectuals, at self-important rebels or reformers, and not to be forgotten, at pitiably cold and arrogant functionaries—upholders at all costs of a sterile status quo.

What are we to do with such a cranky point of view, at once skeptical and innocent? Recommend psychotherapy for this priest? Maybe a stint of "activism"? Maybe a determined effort to rise in the Church's bureaucracy? He is intelligent, alright, and when he wishes, quite appealing, noticeably charming—a real success with certain influential lay people. Good "material" for a monsignor, a bishop! Soon enough, one begins to realize that this "country priest" has a voice utterly foreign to many of us. The voice is that of Bernanos himself, as it comes across in his religious and political writing; and the voice is also that of his other unforgettable fictional creations—as in *Mouchette,* the story of a young woman whose impoverished, vulnerable innocence makes her, at once, a judge of all of us and a victim whose brief life ends in horrible despair. This authorial voice, calling from another time (Bernanos died in 1948) and another place (he was a fervent apostle of French traditionalist culture) turns out to be, in the end, a voice fiercely anxious to summon the spirit of the early Christian Church, which was defiantly egalitarian, brazenly indifferent to the various "principalities and powers."

Bernanos scorned what I suppose has to be called our modern knowledge—that mix of social consciousness, psychological sophistication, and cultural experimentation which so many of us proudly claim as our liberating heritage. Neither Marx nor Freud meant all that much to him. He had no great faith in secular progress—in the liberal state as the Great Benefactor. He was originally a conservative royalist, but he turned against that political position also—especially during the Spanish Civil War, when he saw murderous greed to be the property of everyone, including priests and nuns, never mind wealthy landowners and industrialists. He had spotted, early on, the hypocrisies and arrogant, self-important postures of the well-to-do, agnostic intellectuals who placed every emphasis on mental exploration and statist intervention and radical change in the way people get on personally (with respect to their family life, their sexual life, their social habits and cultural preferences). Suddenly, late in life, he turned on the conservative bourgeoisie—and yes, on his own beloved Catholic Church: all in the name of Jesus Christ (an ancient rabbi who spoke with the voice of Jeremiah and Isaiah and Amos, an itinerant teacher and healer who was scorned by church and state alike, who died in extreme poverty and social exile), because in His name a worldwide collection of rich and powerful people, loaded with property and jewels and extravagant possessions of all kinds, fight for their own continued power and privilege. How he detested the betrayal of the Holy Roman Catholic Church from within—the gold and diamonds it holds, the ermine-lined cloaks of its big-deal princes, their palaces and castles and luxury cars and unceasing display of money and acquisitions. His country curé, his young woman, Mouchette, his historical favorite, Jeanne d'Arc—indeed, all his heroes and heroines—were, really, aspects of one image: that of our Lord—our suffering, scorned, abandoned, betrayed, yet ineffably triumphant Lord. Our Lord who obtained just about everyone's back of the hand, and yet held on for the sake of all of us. His purpose: to become, once and for all, our never-ending companion in the experience of this earthly life.

For Bernanos, Christ is both served by the Church and abandoned by its members, even as He was by His disciples. Each day, Bernanos knew, the Church (as with all of us who claim allegiance to Him) achieves exemplary faithful moments, but alas, falls under spells of scandal. No wonder Bernanos is hard to classify. He was a radical traditionalist, a conservative communitarian, an intensely Catholic layman who grieved hard for his Church's continuing sins. He was a fiery and fussy individual who searched throughout his life for a community of Christian believers—and died very much alone, yearning with all his heart and soul for release from us, yearning with extreme anticipation for the sight of Him.

January–February 1983

"Working My Burden"

A black tenant farmer he was, then, in 1967, when I first met him, and a black tenant farmer he still is today. But time takes its toll, he reminded me recently, as we reminisced together. I had returned to Alabama in the summer, a whirl of a trip, all too characteristic of my ilk—the busy, self-importance of the Yankee bourgeoisie. He had no claim to being in a rush; his time was mine, all of it I wanted, and then some. As for my various obligations, he sure hoped they didn't "overwhelm" me. I thanked him for his concern, and hastened (in a hurry with words, also!) to let him know that I was "alright." I was referring to my body—letting him know that I wasn't suffering any ill effects, as a consequence of my various speedy trips. But he had other thoughts in mind, and he was willing to offer them without hesitation: "You can get going so fast, you lose your way. Jesus told us: He said, *He's* the way, but we figure *we're* the way, and that's being lost!"

Suddenly, I felt less hurried, less harried, but more anxious. In a moment, I was annoyed: what has my "schedule" got to do with such a remark? I'd already seen two biblical warnings on the road— urgent ones, announcing that "the wages of sin is death"; and now I was getting another one!

Yes, the Bible Belt! Yes, the unchanging rural South, black and white alike! It is different, up there at secular Harvard, where "moral reasoning" is studied hard, and God is "a notion of tran-scendence"—so I heard Him recently called in a conversation held by two professors who, for sure, knew that Alabama is in the Southeastern part of the United States, and that blacks "down there" have lots of problems.

As for Joshua Travis, my black yeoman friend, he must have seen a bad mood cross my face as I wondered at whom to direct my spleen: Dixie pietists, ever ready at the mouth with biblical admonitions, or big-deal professors from New England college towns, ever ready with smart talk. Mr. Travis urged a Coke on me, and I sat down and loosened my tie, and he talked some more: "It's only a short time He put us here, and we can't be expected to remember every day *why* we're here, only once in a while. Mostly, my mind is on the weather, and the land—my crops. Come Sunday, I try to pay my respects to Jesus Christ, our Lord, but I'll bet you one thing: no one's fooling Him, including Joshua Travis, when he asks for a good soak of a rain to fall on Alabama, and the price of cotton to go up, and the price of fertilizer to go down. No sir, there must be lots of laughs up in Heaven on Sundays when the prayers start flooding in from all over, and people are asking for this, for that, and they're so Christian, they say, and they're ready to pray and be good, and all they want is a few favors in return.

"A couple of Sundays ago, my wife caught me! I was scribbling a few notes to myself. She said: what you doing—what you writing there, Joshua? I said: I'm just recollecting myself. She said: for whose sake? I said: for my own. She said: if for your own, then why the pencil and the paper? I said: so I won't forget. She said: you don't forget it if you can remember to write it down. I said: sometimes you do. Then we had to go. When we got to church, we was singing and praying and I took out my piece of paper, and she saw me, the wife did, and she shook her head. I went on with my reading my notes, and I was set to put the paper back in my pocket, when she leaned over, she did, and grabbed my notes to herself, and she crumpled them in her big right hand and threw them on the floor, and my daughter started to pick them up, and she whacked her, she did, and I closed my eyes and started to talk with Jesus, because I figured that if I didn't, we'd all be shouting at each other, and the minister would be giving me a sermon—that I'm the devil, and I'd better get out of his church fast, or he'll make sure I spend all of eternity in Hell, chains around my hands and my feet.

"I confessed to Jesus that I was out for myself, like others, and I was sorry. I think I forgot where I was. Suddenly I was standing, and everyone else was sitting, and my wife was saying sit, sit, and I thought she was worried about me, not angry at me, and I was glad. So, I did it; I sat myself down, and I sent Jesus Christ one more message, on the busiest day of the week for Him: please forgive me for being so stuck on myself, and not thinking of You, and all You have to do, never mind Joshua Travis and everyone I know in this county, and my kinfolk in the next county, and up in Birmingham as well.

"The next day, I was walking on the land, and it was sunny, and we'd had a good rain, and I knew the crops were grateful, and I could hear them pushing their way up, yes sir, I could, and I got down on my knees and I was pruning, and getting rid of some weeds, and I thought that since I was down there on the ground, I'd say thank you to Him, and I did: I said, I'm here, and it's Monday, another day for me to be working my burden, and thank you, Jesus Christ Almighty, for giving me a chance to do it—work my burden until you say enough is enough, and it's time to come home. In a few seconds I went on my feet, but I was still lost to the world for a while, except that I watched and watched two dogs and they fight so bad sometimes, and get so huffy sometimes, you'd think they were human beings."

By then my bottle of Coke had been consumed, and the heat of a particular summer day had made my shirt wet all over, and I felt myself conscious of my watch—at first, because the band was soaked with sweat, and needed some drying out, but soon enough, because the small hand had moved along, and not far away a plane would be waiting, and a passenger had to get on it, lest a lecture the next day not be given. So, I said goodbye, and Joshua Travis replied with, "God be with you," and I thought to myself: he means it, and that being the case, no wonder I felt the authority in his voice, almost as if, I believed, God *would* be with me, on that man's, Joshua Travis's, account.

March 1983

Remembering Dorothy Day
Yet Again

During the 1950s, while a medical student at Columbia University's College of Physicians and Surgeons, I would do volunteer work at a Catholic Worker "hospitality house" in Manhattan. I got to know Dorothy Day fairly well during those years, and kept up with her until the last, tiring months of her life kept her from most of her old friends. Few weeks pass that I don't think of her—the example she offered all of us of a faith in God constantly tested by a commitment to living as Jesus, God become flesh, chose to live: among the poor, the vulnerable, the marginal, the sick of mind and heart. Sometimes I find myself being in simple awe of her—that she could resist so long and hard the blandishments of this secular, materialist society, especially compelling to her, surely, because for many years before her conversion to Catholicism she lived a 20th-century American life, the radical intellectual version, to the full. At other times I feel her taking after me, telling me I ought not think this or say that or do whatever it is I've just done—have the comfortable, satisfying time of a member of the 20th-century American bourgeoisie. There are still other moments when her personal grace, her continuing charity toward others, seem hopelessly distant, and therefore forbidding and intimidating to the rest of us sinners.

She would have patience with none of the above inclinations of my mind (and I suspect I'm not alone in the way I've often reacted to her, to others of moral or religious significance who have shared this century with us). She once told me this: "I'm tired of hearing myself called 'saintly.' Such a way of disregarding what we all have to do in our own ways—follow God's lead! To call me 'saintly' is to rob and cheat me—of my very humanity! I am as mean and nasty in my head and my heart as all the rest of us here. Every day we fail spiritually. Who is an exception to that—who gets an A plus in the eyes of God? Not me! Just this morning, I was thinking of someone I know with a terrible anger and scorn in my heart! I tried to forget the person; I worked on the soup line, serving others in order to help myself a little!"

At the time I was rather entranced with psychiatric interpretation as a mode of life (not to mention a mode of faith!). I took note of a rather stern, unrelenting conscience—wondered, after the fashion of the psychiatrists I was meeting in medical school courses, why this decent and kind woman was being so hard on herself. Words or expressions such as "masochism" or "irrational guilt" crossed my psychologically feverish mind. I wondered how serving a large number of down-and-out Bowery folk would help someone like her who seemed so sensitive to her own failings, which are inevitable in all of us. Moreover, I was convinced that Dorothy Day's moment of dissatisfaction with another person was justified by what that person had said or done. Don't we all need to "express" our anger?

Years later, when I was talking with Dorothy Day in a somewhat more formal way, interviewing her for an essay I was attempting on the Catholic Worker Movement, I told her that I couldn't get the above-mentioned moment out of my head. She smiled. She remained silent a bit longer than was her usual habit. She spoke slowly, tersely: "We are here because *we* are in need. We are here because *we* are hungry. I am always being told how nice it is that *we* feed *them;* but I know in my heart that *we* are being fed all the time, and if it is hard to explain that to others, then we have to keep trying, because Christ asked it of us—the recognition that He is part of suffering, wherever it takes place, and of course, so are we."

A lot of complex theology, and I suppose, psychology, were packed into those words—hers characteristically: plain, strong, unpretentious, and always, it seemed, connected to the life, the words, the advice, and experience of Jesus Christ. She was ever the Christian radical, utterly unwilling to settle for things as they are—or yes, as they appear to be. Let the so-called "world" conclude that she was a saint, or a marvelously generous and idealistic person; and let her also be considered an "odd one" personally—well-educated and easily able to get a good job, a proper job (as, say, a newspaper reporter, teacher, essayist, or novelist). Let that same "world" fret about her "behavior," and always, her "motives," her "problems," her "personality." Let some of us who worry about "them," the poor, out of our secular, reforming good will, applaud her for her intentions—even as, in our comfortable literary or academic situation, we seek "fundamental" answers, propound the need for "structural" changes, analyze the nature of the "dialectic," or the "historical processes" which have brought us to this or that "state." Let us, really, pat her on the head (while, maybe, wondering about its difficulties) and indeed pat the entire Catholic Worker Movement on the head, while hastening to analyze those truly important subjects, those large scale matters (worthy of us, of our time and effort!) such as East-West tensions or the question of "productivity" in America, in Europe, in the entire world.

And while we do all those important tasks, write our articles and books, prepare our theses, our position papers, and make our analyses, she and her co-workers—"fools for Christ"—have continued to make the soup daily, have offered it to others, have taken it to their own lips as well, have said their prayers, have lowered their heads in this room or that, at one church or another, hoping and praying for God's forgiveness—for themselves, never mind any one of the handy "thems" we all can find to scorn, or, yes, even to pity and patronize. She could never forget (I well remember!) the question asked by that great master of reality Joseph Stalin: "The Pope—how many divisions has he?" For her there was another reality, not that of the Gulag's death camps, not that of nuclear missiles, nor that of posh shops or clever wordy ideas thrown like crumbs to readers and listeners. "God has given us a moment," I heard her once say, "to be worthy of His love." She paused, then added this: "That is what we must do, all our lives, in every way possible, until He calls us back."

April 1983

Orwell's Decency

As we approach the year 1984, the name George Orwell comes to mind more and more among many—and comes to print, as well. He is being claimed by conservatives, or reclaimed by the political Left, to which he by and large belonged during his rather short (47 years) lifetime. His novel *1984* has, of course, occasioned this accession of attention, and too, this tug-of-war; but Orwell (a pseudonym for Eric Blair, by background of Eton and of England's clergy and commercial class) has not lacked for attention since— well, 1948, certainly, when he published a novel whose title was, quite simply, a reversal of that year's last two digits. By then, actually, he'd already created a considerable stir with *Animal Farm* (1945), a novel meant to remind us that bestiality is very much part of our condition. Indeed, the novel stresses an irony others have declared over the centuries—for example, Orwell's English predecessors the English Romantics: we human beings, creatures of intentionality, have used words such as "bestial" or "animal" as a means of fobbing off our own wicked, greedy, cruel instincts on an unwilling "them," all of those "inferiors" who live in the forest we supposedly left for good a while back. If Wordsworth celebrated "nature," so did Orwell, in his own way.

For years before those two novels were published Orwell had shown a great commitment to the poor, the weak, the vulnerable. His *Down and Out in Paris and London* (1933) was the result of several years of intense and compassionate observations of hurt and all too pitiable men, women, children. Before that book was written he had lived in the slums of two great capital cities; he had worked as a dishwasher, a kitchen porter; he had come to know tramps and hop-pickers and ordinary folk who worked in factories or small shops, as clerks and hospital orderlies and salespersons. His *The*

Road to Wigan Pier (1937) gave an account of a specially hard-pressed population of workers, England's depression-era coal miners. In that book, too, Orwell's sympathies are obvious, and at times provocative; he admires the strength, the endurance, the stoic everyday courage of the men he came to know both above and below the Lancashire and Yorkshire ground, but he has scant charity for those better off, be they boarding-house owners or, yes, socialist intellectuals (such as those, presumably, of the Left Book Club) who, in fact, had commissioned his inquiry.

In *The Road to Wigan Pier* he rails against the smugness and arrogance of Britain's 1930's political radicals, accuses them of being at an all too instructive remove from working people, who become for so many theorists of the dialectic mere objects in a grand scheme of things—the "one-dimensional" ones whom a Herbert Marcuse and his small cadre of the cognoscenti are meant to lead into some happy world which has emerged clean and pure, despite a few spells of intermediate statism. By 1938, as a matter of fact, Orwell had foreseen what dictators such as Joseph Stalin, or more recently, the Jaruzelskis and Honneckers of our time, and their rather too willing functionaries (and scholarly and literary apologists) are all about. He had gone to fight in Spain, witnessed the betrayal of socialist ideals, and rendered his observations (and strong moral feelings) in *Homage to Catalonia,* a devastating account of political betrayal, of evil masquerading under the banner of egalitarian aspiration.

It was in Orwell's nature to be an ethically alert and active person; but he was also a skeptical rationalist, quick to spot the fake, the dishonest, the pretentious. He had no patience with those who romanticize the poor. He saw that poverty can debase people, turn them into monstrous exploiters of one another. He had even less patience, naturally, with the wealthy and powerful, or the high falutin' academic world, or the self-important literary one, because he knew that their sins of omission and commission were plentiful, and bore the additional burden that goes with privilege: not only a responsibility avoided but a capability shunned to extend help to others far less comfortable. He ended up a loner, disgusted with Tory Britain, yet thoroughly troubled by England's postwar socialist crowd, among whom, he knew, could be found any number of self-centered, condescending, willfully manipulative, and tricky characters. He had no great love for America's conquering materialism, but Lord, he saw Stalinist Russia to be Hell itself. A cranky eccentric with respect to "principalities and powers," he had, nevertheless, become an increasingly celebrated writer, hailed at the end of his life, he himself knew, by the wrong crowd for the wrong reason, for his anti-Stalinism was never meant to give courage to those who cared not a whit about the fate of working-class people in contemporary industrial societies.

One of his most interesting essays was written in 1939 and titled "Charles Dickens"; it is Orwell at his critical and humane best. He writes as no fool about the limits of 19th-century sentimentality (even when expended with kind purpose upon the poor), but also as no fool about some of this century's hard-nosed, insistently practical movers and shakers:

> most revolutionaries are potential Tories, because they imagine that everything can be put right by altering the *shape* of society; once that change is effected, as it sometimes is, they see no need for any other. Dickens has not this kind of coarseness. The vagueness of his discontent is the mark of its permanence. What he is out against is not this or that institution, but as Chesterton put it, "an expression on the human face." Roughly speaking, his morality is the Christian moralist's, but in spite of his Anglican upbringing he was essentially a Bible-Christian, as he took care to make plain when writing his will.

Earlier on, Orwell had declared Dickens's "criticism of society" to be "almost exclusively moral." At another point Orwell says this about Dickens: "Where he is Christian is in his quasi-instinctive siding with the oppressed against the oppressors. As a matter of course he is on the side of the underdog, always and everywhere."

So with Orwell, too; he was a writer whose purposes were essentially those of moral instruction. He was more comfortable, personally, one suspects, with his penniless or hard-up slum companions than with those big shots who wanted to wine and dine him in the last years of his life—when, anyway, he was quite sick, dying the slow death of tuberculosis. An essential decency in him has been much remarked, and without question it made up a big part of his character. Those of us who worship a God, who, when among us, was born among "underdogs" and Himself died one, a declared criminal crucified in order to be rid of, must surely take to Orwell's particular decency—and even dare describe it as Christian in nature, as he does with his moral predecessor, Charles Dickens.

May 1983

James Agee's Religious Sensibility

When my wife and I lived and worked in the changing, even agitated South of the early 1960s we found ourselves constantly thinking of James Agee—especially his thoroughly idiosyncratic, brilliant, vexing, provocative *Let Us Now Praise Famous Men,* an effort to render what he calls the "human actuality" to which he and Walker Evans bore witness. They were, initially, emissaries of Henry R. Luce's *Fortune,* intent on doing a reportorial piece on Alabama tenant farm life of the mid-1930s. (They never did write that piece.) We were, ourselves, trying to understand the lives of some of the South's especially hard-pressed people, and Agee's example seemed instructive and heroic: the willingness to evoke the complexity of things, rather than settle for one or another ideological point of view; and too, the continual, if at times overwrought self-scrutiny which demanded of the reader a similar inclination to question motives, beliefs, purposes.

Moreover, the language of the book is truly exalted, a strong lyrical poetry harnessed to the task of documentary evocation. The language is also stately and biblical—reminiscent of the Book of Common Prayer, which Agee knew well from his childhood. We could find him, at times, self-preoccupied or cursed by what the Church Fathers called scrupulosity—an excessive regard for what is or is not proper, as in St. Paul's well-known comparison of "the letter" as against "the spirit." But we were never bored with his mind at work. He waged a serious struggle on behalf of the dignity he believed present in his tenant farmer hosts, and doing so he was at all times assisted by a grand and arresting writer's skill. No one has accomplished what Agee did in *Let Us Now Praise Famous Men*—connect the lives of a region's poor folk to the West's entire intellectual and moral tradition.

The title of the book was no mere catchy afterthought of the author's. The title comes from the introductory words of Chapter 44 of Ecclesiasticus, a part of the Apocrypha; and at one moment in the book, 14 of that Chapter's 23 sections are offered the reader, a summary statement placed solemnly and boldly on a full page. Agee's own difficult battle to make sense of this life's meaning was, of course, a continuing one; but he was never more intensely absorbed in ethical reflection than at this time, his late 20s. (He died at only 45 of a heart attack.) Before he went to Alabama he was much preoccupied with poetry, and afterwards he would turn to movie criticism and film script writing (all the while working on a novel, which would only be published posthumously), but his experience in Alabama made his mind attend the so-called "existentialist" questions, even as he was perceptive and generous enough to realize that not only big-deal, self-important intellectuals pay those same questions serious and continuing heed. Why not, then, turn to Ben Sirach's wonderously wise counsel, so similar in many respects to some of the greatest Hebrew gifts to all of us, the Proverbs and the Psalms? Why not let the Jewish teacher of the first quarter of the second century B.C. instruct Agee's readers as had once been the case of ancient Jerusalem's people—teach the virtues of humble association, across age and time and sect and class, with those "famous men" who were, indeed, "merciful," and whose "righteousness" ought not be forgotten, no matter that they "have no memorial"?

No question Agee's reflective side was deeply nourished by his life. He was Tennessee-born, and an important part of his childhood and early youth was spent at the Saint Andrew's School, where (near Sewanee in the Cumberland Plateau) boys boarded under the watchful religious scrutiny of the Monastic Order of the Holy Cross (Episcopalian). (He lost his father at the age of seven.) Later, there would be Exeter and Harvard and New York's proudly cosmopolitan agnostic world of Greenwich Village and *Partisan Review;* and much liquor and three marriages and friendships with writers, actors, movie directors, photographers; and liberal politics and a love of jazz and all-night talk, and ambitious dreams, projects, cultural involvements—writing the words for the *African Queen,* imagining a movie that captured the wild, extravagantly self-indulgent yet meditative quality of Gauguin's Tahiti life, keeping up with the likes of Charles Chaplin and John Huston.

Time somewhat squandered, many of us might say. Certainly Agee lived too fast, died too young. Still, a headlong rush, it seemed, toward departure from this life characterized only one part of his nature; he was also a man of religious sensibility (I do not say, obviously, religious faith). His letters to Father Flye, an Episcopal priest and friend from childhood to the day of the last breath, reveal a talented writer all too entranced, perhaps, with the blandishments of America's mid-20th century secular culture; but also reveal a man deeply aching for some larger view and explanation of this earthly trial:

> In other words, God is not a sentimental anarchist who decides to play poker when a bad hand at gin rummy has been dealt. He knows, sees, and cares what is happening; and the tests, the relationship of all of it to God, remain vivid and unfathomable; but He does not interfere with the laws of Nature (which as their creator He gave autonomy), or with the human laws of creation or self-destruction (ditto).

Nor were these idle or stray thoughts. The title of his one, fine book of poems is *Permit Me Voyage*, and one feels, in reading young Agee's lyrical vision (which won for him a Yale Younger Poets award, at the age of only 25), a deep hesitation before the great mysteries—those Gauguin condensed into the questions placed upon his famous Triptych of 1897: Where do we come from? What are we? Where are we going? Then, there was *Morning Watch* (1951), a novella which explores the emergence of self-awareness as, at once, an emotional and sexual but—very important—also a moral and religious matter; and the location for such investigation is a religious school, the time: Easter week, Good Friday to be precise. Finally, the novel *A Death in The Family*, which won him acclaim and prizes after he left us (was called from us), had a strong autobiographical strain, and centers on not only the meaning of a parent's death to a child, but the nature of the Church as it, too, grapples with such an event. Agee scorns a certain Episcopalian haughtiness and pride—but the vehemence, one feels, reflects a Christian awareness that God's grace may be mediated through earthly institutions (sometimes) but is never to be equated with their (inevitably) flawed character.

I remember, in 1964, a black high school student, a member of the sit-in movement, saying this to my wife and me about James Agee: "I've been looking at your copy of *Let Us Now Praise Famous Men,* and a lot of it I can't figure out. But he sure was searching, and I guess it was for God, the way he writes. I sure hope God smiled on him when he showed up before Him." My wife nodded, and so did I—and yes, we still "sure hope" that such was and ever more will be the case for James Agee.

June 1983

Suffering and Faith

I write these words during Lent—to be exact, a few days before Good Friday. I remember well Lenten seasons of my childhood— the children who came to grade school with ashes on their fore- heads: a mark of their kinship in grave suffering, and of course, their connection with the Roman Catholic Church. My closest childhood friend suggested two years in a row that I accompany him, obtain ashes for my forehead. I remember asking: "Would I then be a Catholic?" He was sure the answer was yes. My parents, of course, had other ideas! But I do remember their intrigue— inevitable, I suppose—with that explicit and personal identification of Catholic parishioners with the extreme travail of Jesus Christ. I also remember my father's cynicism: "Those ashes disappear quickly, and so does the goodness they are meant to inspire."

Even then I wondered if it was "goodness" that was at stake—or whether the New England agnostic stoicism of a parent wasn't being imposed on quite another tradition. I remember my friend's mother, who had in her living room two pictures of the Bleeding Heart of Jesus (the 1940s!) sending this message through me, back home: "The ashes remind us of the suffering we all experience, and Jesus died to redeem that suffering." My father was singularly unimpressed. He wasn't sure the message was theologically correct; and he certainly felt no need to be reminded of mankind's suffering. Hitler was then in control of most of Europe.

Later, at college, I would study with Perry Miller, who had his own struggles with religion: a strong interest in America's Puritan (17th- and 18th-century) culture set against a worldly, intellectual 20th-century skepticism, not to mention the experience of military service in Europe during the Second World War. I remember him telling me this—words my father would have found congenial, indeed: "I was one of the first to arrive at the [concentration] camp. To my last day on earth I'll remember the scene. I looked up at the sky, and saw a beautiful sunny day. God seemed nowhere in evidence! A soldier next to me must have been having the same thoughts; he said to me: 'I can't believe any God would tolerate this.' I nodded, and then I thought of the Crucifixion. I was going to remind the fellow—remind myself!—that Jesus had gone through a terrible death, too. But somehow I couldn't say a word. It seemed obscene—to compare *anything*, even the holy moment of Christianity, to this nightmare, this hell, we had stumbled into. Then another soldier, I'll never forget him, got down on his knees and started praying. He had his rosary beads in his hands. His gesture broke the ice for all of us. Others got down and prayed with him. Some of us—me included—stood with our heads bowed."

Perry Miller spoke those words over and over again, in large lecture halls and seminar rooms and the privacy of his Widener study. He also wrote those words down. I think of them every Good Friday, when I sit in some church, some place, wondering about things—God's eternal mysteries and our never ending questions, not to mention the terrifying events which keep prompting those questions. I also think of a child migrant farmworker I knew in the mid-1960s, a girl of 10 who had already learned how to pick beans and pick tomatoes and pick low-lying oranges and lemons. She had heard, many times, an especially insistent evangelical minister give his impromptu sermons among people such as her parents, and she had watched some of those people (but not her mother and father) approach that man and tell him yes, by all means yes, they wanted to sign up, "enlist in Christ's army," as he told them they were doing. The child admired her parents for their considered hesitation. She also asked herself why they were so reluctant to embrace what others found ever so comforting. In turn, I asked her for her thoughts on their thoughts. Shrewdly, she asked me for my own thoughts. I demurred—not, I hope, out of sly prurience, a substantial hazard of my ilk, but rather a strong confusion that goes way back in its origin (as I've just tried to indicate). She didn't go much for my protestations, which were put this way, I recall: "I don't know what to say. I think your parents must have their good reasons to stand back and wait, while others don't. Maybe they don't like to hear a sermon out in the fields. Maybe they prefer to go to church."

In fact, she knew her parents were no reliable churchgoers. Often (in warm months) they were "on the road," and working on Sundays. Often (on inclement Sundays) they were tired, and glad to sleep late. But her grandmother's interests and inclinations were another matter—and proved decisively important on this issue before her and me, that day: "My gramma goes to church all the time, and she gets me to go with her a lot. She saw that man preaching, and she didn't like him and she told us why: he's too much stuck on himself. My mother agreed. Gramma likes the ministers who make you want to cry, and not make you think how great you are. She says Jesus cried for everyone, and if you pay attention to Him, you can't help but cry for all the people, everywhere."

She'd made her point, given her explanation—suffering as so utterly central an element of Christ's life, hence of the Christian faith. But the ambitious busybody listener couldn't let the discussion end there—and do his own reflection in response to what he'd heard. He had to do, it seemed, what he'd learned to do—the constraining imperatives of a given professional life. That is to say, he had to ask another question: "Do you think we should really cry for *everyone, everywhere,* according to Jesus?" She didn't stop for more than a few seconds before she gave me this terse, unequivocal reply: "Yes, sir, I do." Again I had to press her—and I now realize, press my own perplexed head: "Well, how about the growers—the ones who own all this?" My right hand moved in an arc—to emphasize the money and power implicit in all that fertile productive land, miles of it stretching to the furthest point in the horizon. She was, yet again, quick to reply, and confidently brief: "Oh yes, them too."

I looked disbelieving, maybe annoyed. I said nothing. I was trying to figure out how further to address her, how to make my various points about injustice and even (I thought) cruel inhumanity. She must have sensed the turmoil of my secular moral life, and she addressed it before I could let it find its own words: "*Especially* you have to cry for the rich, gramma says; they're in the worse trouble of all, Jesus told us." An ensuing silence between us, I still remember, was broken by the importunate demands of her dog that he be allowed outside to run, romp, enjoy an early, warm spring evening.

Edith Stein's Cross

Among the 20th-century conversions to Roman Catholicism, that of Edith Stein is surely one of the most edifying and memorable. She was born in Breslau, Germany, to Jewish parents. Her father was a timber merchant who died when she, his last child, was only two. Her mother took over the business and managed well. She was, however, a woman of divided loyalties—a passionate commitment to the Jewish religion and culture lived uneasily with the requirement of participation in commerce. When Edith Stein was nine the 20th century began—and soon enough her own personal, intellectual, and spiritual journey would intersect with the fate of the German nation.

She was an exceedingly bright child who luckily was not denied the advantages of an excellent education. By the late 19th century Germany's Jews, even the most orthodox, had obtained relatively secure access to a progressive society's schools, not to mention its advanced literary, artistic, and musical life. The ghettos of Europe were elsewhere—to the east, in Poland and Russia. The Germany of Kaiser Wilhelm II was significantly tainted with anti-Semitism, but it was not by any means of a kind to threaten the likes of a gifted, ambitious student such as the young Edith Stein. Moreover, by adolescence she had abandoned Judaism in favor of an agnostic assimilationist posture not at all rare among early 20th-century German Jews.

By 1913 Edith Stein had become a serious student of philosophy, and was studying with Edmund Husserl. His phenomenological mode of inquiry would influence her greatly—and arguably, turn out to be the first major religious influence of her adult life. He had dared object to Kant's continuing hold on so many German philosophers—a stubborn refusal to acknowledge

61

the capacity human beings have to comprehend in a reasonably conclusive way the nature of this world. Husserl, it can be said, embraced with enthusiasm a world shunned by neo-Kantians, for whom thinking—one idea after another, and philosophical systems galore—was the great reality. He saw Truth in "the things of this world," and never for a moment doubted that the here and now of this life was real and knowable. His brilliant assistant, Edith Stein, quickly absorbed that point of view—an important contrast to the hermetic relativism of idealistic philosophy. Her doctoral dissertation, published eventually as a book, *On the Problem of Empathy*, earned her quick recognition as a brilliant scholar, able to negotiate the treacherous and turbid waters of the question of "consciousness." (Quite on her own, incidentally, she postulated the equivalent of the Freudian unconscious, thickly textured in response to childhood experience—in her term "the mode of non-actuality.")

In November of 1917 a dear friend of hers, a fellow philosopher, Adolph Reinach, was killed in military action on the Western front. He and his wife had a year before become Christians—moved from a world of intellectual curiosity to one of communion in Christ's name. Edith Stein mourned the loss of a friend, but could not stop noticing the almost unnerving dignity and composure of his young widow. She was also aware of the conversion of Max Scheler, a fellow philosopher, to Catholicism.

Yet, she came to the Roman Catholic Church—she made quite clear later in life—through a chance meeting with St. Teresa of Avila, whose autobiography happened to be on a bookshelf in the home of friends with whom she was staying. On New Year's day 1922, she was baptized in the Church—and, one gathers, kept thinking thereafter of St. Teresa and her passionate devotion to Jesus. Teresa's exemplary love for God and His Son surely must have served to inspire Edith Stein to go through a dramatic shift in her career; she abandoned an exceptionally promising academic life for one of secondary school teaching and prayer. Like Simone Weil, also a brilliant Jewish-born student of philosophy drawn to Catholicism, Stein found a certain exhilaration in her everyday work with young women—as if now a learned mind had, at last, found itself sprung from the dreary exertions of self-display. She was charged with the responsibility of others: to help them grow morally and educationally, and not least, spiritually. Additionally, she pursued

St. Thomas—ultimately translating into German his *Quaestiones Disputatae de Veritate;* and doing so she rendered significant and clarifying exegesis, thereby becoming (now among Catholic theologians) a formidable intellectual presence.

In early 1933 Hitler (yet another aspect of the Antichrist) took power in Germany, and so Edith Stein (in the Nazi eyes still a Jew) could no longer teach school. For her personally, an ironic moment of eternal good fortune had arrived: she felt free, at last, to apply for admission to the Carmelite Order. When, in a ceremony, she was clothed a nun, prominent intellectuals from all over Germany came to the Cologne Chapel of the Carmelites where the event took place. Germany had already begun its deep descent into Hell, and Edith Stein was prepared to pray fervently and by the hour to the Jesus of the Cross—that He take unto Himself the innocents already being brutally murdered by fascist thugs. Still, the Carmelite Provincial was not quite ready to permit the loss of a shining intellect—especially given the terrible outbursts of irrationality then prevalent. For several years, while Hitler consolidated his murderous hold, Edith Stein prayed, thought, and wrote—and the result was her great study, *Finite and Eternal Being,* published posthumously. She had moved from phenomenology to Christian existentialism.

Meanwhile Germany had moved closer to the lower reaches of the Inferno. By late 1938 the life of Sister Teresa Benedicta of the Cross (Edith Stein's new name) was in distinct jeopardy. On December 31 of that year she was taken across the border to Holland; there she began the last and tragically brief period of her life in the Carmelite community of the town Echt.

For three full years she gave of herself unstintingly—with constant pleas to "the Heart of Jesus," that she be taken "as a sacrifice of expiation for true peace, that the reign of the Antichrist may perish. . . ." She also studied mystical theology, and wrote her final study, a series of reflections on St. John of the Cross, published eventually as *The Science of The Cross.* She was working on that project when (on August 2, 1942) the Nazis came, seized her, and sent her to Auschwitz, where a mere week later she was gassed.

It has been reported that during those last days in the concentration camp she displayed an utter calm—attending the hurt, the sick, the agitated and frightened. Who was this center of stoic prayer and loving-kindness, this incarnation of thoughtfulness, good judgment, and decency—all in the face of imminent death? A splinter of the Cross, surely—an instrument of His grace, His example; and yes, given that awful time, a reminder that Christ was a Jew, and so were His disciples (as St. Paul put it, *Hebraei sunt: et ego*—"they are Jews, and so am I") and so was by ancestry Teresa of Avila, and in their beloved company so was Edith Stein, a proud and talented scholar who threw herself gladly, ecstatically at His feet, He of the Cross, He whose Cross had become her cross.

September 1983

On Abortion

For many years I have struggled hard to figure out what I believe to be the morally correct view with respect to abortion. I am, in that regard, still struggling, and I beg the reader's patience, as I take up this subject, and in future issues other equally controversial matters—on none of which I've written before, because for years my wife and I have talked about them with one another, often with much confusion and many mixed feelings. In any event, this periodical surely invites some written effort to declare one's attitude on moral issues all of us ought consider carefully—and the "Harvard Diary" enables, I believe, the only manner of expression my mind finds unintimidating as it approaches a discussion of abortion, or indeed, school prayer, pornography, homosexuality, and the so-called sexual "liberation" movements, subjects I'd like to discuss in the months ahead.

I am a physician and a psychiatrist, and I have had my share of experiences which keep the mind awake and in some considerable anguish through the nights, never mind working days. I remember, for instance, during my residency years of child psychiatry, admitting a 14-year-old girl to the hospital, who had been raped by a stranger, and who was, needless to say, upset. She was from a devout Catholic family, and they all were stunned, horrified. Yet, she decided she did not want an abortion, nor could her parents find it in themselves to suggest she have one. I was horrified myself—a fine, decent girl, terribly abducted and raped, and now to bear a child she did not "want," only felt she must have out of her religious faith. At the time, the 1950s, she would not, of course, have easily obtained a (legal) abortion: her life was not in danger, nor was she "psychiatrically ill" in any honorable sense of that expression. When the baby was born she signed the little girl over to a church adoption agency, and *then* became extremely upset. I saw her for a year, worked with her as she cried and cried, and asked (in the tradition of Job) haunting, unforgettable questions about what life means, and why we are asked to experience some of its terrible moments.

Such a medical encounter, of course, provides a rather unusual point of departure for any discussion of abortion. We are now in the 1980s, when abortion is, sadly, a fact of our everyday American life. No committee of doctors would be necessary to review that quite young woman's eligibility for a so-called "therapeutic abortion," and Lord knows, given changes (for the worse) in the lives of many American Catholics, one wonders whether she and her parents would now feel as strongly as they once did about the "sinfulness," as they then put it, of abortion. As for myself, I have to declare, candidly, the direction of my own thinking: back then I wondered why in the world this "child," as she seemed, and in many ways was, couldn't have an immediate abortion, then later work out her "feelings," as my kind drearily put it—along with, it seems, everyone who writes in those "Living" sections of our papers, and everyone who reads what is written there and elsewhere (all the awful books telling people to pay attention, pay infinite attention to their, again, "feelings"). Now I think I would sit in awe of that youth's, that family's considerable courage and integrity— and consider myself blessed by God to be in the position of listening to them, learning from them, never mind trying to be of some personal help to them.

I suppose I am trying to say this: I can't forget other women I've met who, unlike the person cited above, did not at all want to persist with a pregnancy initiated by virtue of rape; I can't forget—a much larger number—the women I've met, and others I know who (out of ignorance and desperation and confusion and plain wantonness and carelessness) have ended up pregnant, and had no interest or desire to carry that pregnancy to term, and have shown every promise, alas, of being as indifferent to their children as they obviously were to their own personal, never mind moral, obligations; and not least, I can't forget what I've seen in this country among the poor, and especially abroad, in the *favellas* of Rio de Janeiro, for example, where I've come to know women who have had no education and are barely alive themselves and who have no prospects, it seems, none at all, and who have child after child, all going hungry and malnourished—women for whom, they keep telling me, bearing yet another child is a terrible, aching tragedy. Yet those women know not how to stop becoming pregnant, nor is anyone around anxious to (or, it seems, able to) help them with their awful situation, including (they also tell me) the particular priests and nuns whose church is at the foot of this or that *favella*, and who denounce abortion, yet witness without apparent despair children dying of untreated diseases, children in pain because their stomachs are empty, and with them their jobless, bewildered parents. "I see an ocean of children here, to match the ocean that pounds the Copacabana," one *favellado* told me, and then she added, "I become pregnant with the children, and they die inside me or die outside, and only three have lived to be over 10, and if I live to be old and stop having children it will be because God wants me to have time to cry and cry for all those I've had and lost."

I also can't forget what I see all around me now—abortion become an everyday fact of life, a mere routine, and oh dear God, a "right," part of the program of "entitlement" a self-centered population utterly demands. I can't forget an obscenity I heard a patient tell a group of doctors—after the advice she received from a "counsellor" that she "not worry," that a "procedure" would quickly "be done," and that there would be soft music and an "upbeat" atmosphere: she fled in moral horror. How I wish this world were different—that life were regarded by all of us as the Divine gift that it is: in the *favellas* of Rio de Janeiro, in the slums of our own cities, and not least, in the comfortable homes and apartments of our upper-middle class liberal voting suburbs, where the bottom line is, I fear, not God's words, not even a powerfully convincing moral code, but the urges and requirements of something called "the personality": what will the pregnancy *mean* to her, or does she *want* the child, or how will she *feel* as a result of this *experience*? A matter, one begins to realize, of egoism given a social and cultural *carte blanche*.

What to say about what one holds to be true? I believe with no special or surprising insight, that an abortion willfully terminates a life—and that it is God almighty who has given us, each and every one of us, this life. An abortion, then, is not only an utter tragedy but an affront to the Lord—as is all death which mankind visits upon itself, sometimes with the indifference or tragic acquiescence of our various churches: wars, the infant mortality that goes with poverty, the killing diseases that millions and millions of suffering, vulnerable children (and their parents) have to take for granted as inevitable, because there is no work, inadequate food, no medical care of any consequence.

Abortion, then, is an aspect of our utter sinfulness toward ourselves, toward others. Abortion as an acceptable part of a well-to-do nation's legal and cultural life is a measure of how far we have come from a reigning spiritual life. In one way or another, through greed and aggressive manipulations and callousness and self-serving rationalizations, we shun our obligations to others: that they, too, live, and be regarded by ourselves a part of not only this family, or that neighborhood, or region, nation, continent—but, more than anything else, God's community, to which, inside or outside the womb, all life belongs. If we are to make "exceptions," as we do with "honorable wars," say, or self-defense, and with pregnant women themselves in danger of dying, and any other particular example, then we have to do so with aching agony, with reverent reflection, with an awareness of our constant temptation to the sin of pride (in the form of smugness, arrogance, vulgar self-interest) and not least with sustained prayer.

October 1983

On School Prayer

All during my school years, elementary and secondary, I remember those first minutes of the day, Monday through Friday from September to June: we arrive in the classroom, we sit down and are called to order, our teacher reads to us from the Bible, we pray, then we stand and salute the flag, and to it and our country pledge our allegiance. When my own children came of school age I was utterly amazed to learn that none of that routine was to be theirs. School prayers were not for the offspring of the liberal intelligentsia, nor saluting the flag. What if there were a child in the classroom who had his doubts about the existence of God? What if, indeed, his or her parents were convinced atheists, and have taught him or her a similar line of thinking? What about the First Amendment, and the Supreme Court's rulings?

As for the flag, when my children had started school the American flag, in one sad and thoroughly obnoxious display after another, was being dragged through the streets, spat upon, desecrated, mocked. Should children be "indoctrinated," I began to hear asked, in "vulgar nationalism" (one remark I heard in a New England town meeting in 1970), or in "chauvinism," another description I heard compared unfavorably to—well, "the philosophy of spaceship earth," which urges commitment to what the speaker called "a larger entity"? Only to such "entities" ought we "feel loyalty," he kept insisting.

At the time and later, I was more than a little perplexed by my own conflicts as to what and whom I should "feel loyalty." I had been much involved in the civil rights struggles of the early 1960s, and I had been saddened and angered by the way both Democrats and Republicans (Johnson and Nixon) were conducting our various adventures abroad, in Vietnam, Chile, the Philippines, and yes,

69

Central America: a sad spectacle of collusion with awful, awful "principalities and powers," all in the name of an "anti-Communism" which itself helps maintain or generates corrupt statist oligarchies. Meanwhile, there is the horror of so-called "Communism"—the dictatorships that control Poland and Rumania and Czechoslovakia and, not least, Cuba; and of course, the horror of the murderous sponsor, the band in charge of the Kremlin. But as I come up with this recitation, I feel, yet again, a surge of gratitude for being an American—that I don't live in a totalitarian country, whether of the "Right" or the "Left," that even with the serious flaws in America's foreign policy, it is a country I can deeply love, and toward which I can "feel loyalty."

When I saw people in the "peace movement" desecrate the flag, call our leaders "fascist pigs," scream epithets at the country, I was disgusted—even as I kept noticing how mean-spirited, how lacking in "peace" some of those demonstrations were, and how arrogant and smug some of the upper-middle class protesters were about a "them," the poor, benighted working people of this country who still believed (so I heard it put, with sneers) in "Mother, God, Apple Pie, and the Flag." I love apple pie and love my mother; I was taught to respect the flag, feel great affection for my country (one form of affection, my parents taught me, is criticism); and last but not at all least, I happen to believe in God.

Why cannot my children say a prayer in school? Why cannot their teachers do so likewise? Would it really unsettle our Constitution, or some children whose parents don't believe in God, if others for a minute or two lowered their heads in silent acknowledgment of Him, or in explicit prayers to Him? All the time my children and I have to put up with the assaults upon our values, our beliefs, our sense of propriety or decency, and do so often enough in suffering silence—the price of living in a democracy, we're told by civil libertarians, some of them quite predictable in their wordy, public posturing. But when it comes to children praying in school, a tradition in this country that goes back to the early days of the Republic, to the beginning of our schools, we hear of the potential jeopardy to . . . whom?

The jeopardy to the "emotions" of the lonely dissenting child, I assume. (What about the "emotions" of thousands and thousands of children who want to pray but are told no?) The jeopardy, also, to people that would occur in a school district if a "fanatic" religion were to take over, insist upon using the classrooms to spread its interpretation of the Bible, and exclude recognition of all other kinds. To be sure, any halfway decent or honorable pedagogical principle, or custom, or practice, in and out of the classroom, can become corrupted, turned into an instrument of devilish, persecutory self-righteousness. The history of Christianity—the schisms and sectarian struggles and terrible wars—offers proof enough of that danger. Yet, ought we allow the potential excesses this life offers us, with respect to any of our deeds, prevent us from going forth, taking life's risks, getting on with the business of living, part of which, for millions and millions of people, has involved the acknowledgment of Him—as the Declaration of Independence itself does when it refers to the Creator, and as our very currency does with the phrase "In God We Trust"? Will we soon have a case before the Supreme Court demanding that none of us be subject to the potential emotional stress (or personal affront) of using dollar bills that have the above-mentioned phrase printed on them?

As I hear (or in books, see) myself and some of my colleagues strutting about, playing God with others by the hour, demanding the faith of listeners or readers as we tell them this, insist upon that (and Lord save them if they don't embrace our theories speedily enough), I can't help but believe we wouldn't profit enormously from a few minutes a day of heads bowed, while we heed the words of Jeremiah and Isaiah and Amos and surely Ecclesiastes, or the Preacher, not to mention Jesus of Nazareth and His Disciples, each and every one of whom speaks to us in the Bible. We who preach without knowing or acknowledging it in this secular world—one self-confident, if not thoroughly haughty and presumptuous pronouncement after another—might well profit from a moment or longer of daily self-subjugation before the mysteries of this universe; profit from contemplation of the Holy Faith which over many centuries has been part of the life of so many nations and peoples, our own included.

Did not the very settlement of the country have to do, ironically, with the issue of religious faith—the rights of people to worship Him strongly, persistently, seriously. Oh, I'm sure dozens of constitutional theorists and political scientists may come at me as a result of the foregoing with cross looks on their faces and intimidating logic on their tongues and alarm in the tone of their speech. But I sorely regret the absence of school prayers in our schools, and I regret, too, that in many schools I've visited, all over this country, not only are prayers "out" (by law), but the salute to the flag has disappeared, too. For me that salute always conjures up Abraham Lincoln at Gettysburg, a private fantasy, I suppose; and the thought of prayers of children in school—why, they conjure up memories of what a teacher used to tell us in the fifth grade, as we lowered our heads: "We have a chance now to be humble before God, and let's hurry and use that chance!"

November 1983

On Pornography

Recently in a town outside Boston, a number of men and women have been marching in protest, day after day, outside a so-called bookstore. It is a place where all sorts of sex magazines and manuals and slides and films can be purchased—a center of pornographic "materials" set in the middle of what used to be an old New England farming village, and is now a suburb where families try to live a reasonably decent and honorable life. The persistence of the picketing attracted some local news coverage, and soon enough one saw on television one's fellow citizens—ordinary human beings outraged that such a place should be within walking distance of groceries and the post office and, not least, churches. One read comments in the papers on the question: Why must this be tolerated, under what set of laws? On television, and in those papers, one began to hear the answers—the familiar responses of lawyers and so-called "libertarians." The First Amendment was mentioned again and again: we must preserve freedom of speech, freedom of the press; we must beware of setting ourselves up as holier-than-thou judges of others. We must beware of our self-righteousness, because one day's assault on the owners of a shop full of smut might turn into the next day's persecution of those of this or that religious persuasion or intellectual point of view.

I am sure there is some reason always to be watchful, lest intolerance, bigotry, narrow-mindedness, and self-righteous arrogance make serious inroads upon our cultural and, indeed, personal lives. Salem (with its history of witch hysteria) is not all that removed from the particular town, Stoughton, whose struggle I've just mentioned. Religious belief has certainly been used in the past as an excuse to brand people not only witches, but enemies of the state, who must be banished at all costs. Our nation's history offers

73

abundant instances of fearful, frenzied name calling—enough of them, certainly, to give pause to anyone who wants to go after someone else's written or spoken opinions, or yes, personal tastes. In 19th-century Boston nuns were attacked, priests villified. In 20th-century Boston Jews were set upon, beaten. Boston's recent racial history—the violence which daily persists between blacks and whites—has earned the city a sad reputation, indeed. A city whose abolitionists preached loudly to the South is now a city beset by terrible antagonisms grounded in the social and economic vulnerability that so often generates a fearful distrust of others, different by virtue of race, religion, or ethnic background.

I go into the preceding discussion to acknowledge its significance—and because the people of the greater Boston area were asked to remember such matters of law, politics, and history (by one or another voice of legal or constitutional authority) as they contemplated the continuing picketing of the "bookstore." We were warned that our cherished liberty includes the liberty of those who want to buy such things, and the liberty of those who want to sell books, magazines, and pamphlets that appeal to "certain kinds of people."

A friend of mine, a reporter, showed me a representative array of that store's wares, and I thought all I saw to be obscene, tawdry, disgusting. But then, I find myself making similar judgments on magazines such as *Hustler* and *Penthouse,* and they are staples of many American newsstands, not to mention drugstores or even grocery markets. I have to wonder, sometimes, if I'm becoming an old prude. I have to wonder if my reactions (dismay, outrage) to what increasingly we all now can see at the movies or even on television don't mark me as hopelessly puritanical and old-fashioned—as I see sexuality turned into a harsh, manipulative, crudely calculated or promiscuous, violent or bizarre phenomenon. The "old days," we're told, are gone: no more is there effective "censorship" of the movies, and year by year we witness a more "relaxed" standard for the afternoon "soaps" and the evening "sitcoms." As for the magazines, their sense of propriety and decency seems utterly nonexistent.

It has only been a quarter of a century or so that such has been the case—the appearance of a literature of polymorphous perversity, it might well be called. That phrase, "polymorphous perversity," is one I saw and heard used when I was learning to be a psychiatrist—and has to do with the psychological development of young children, their fantasies: a passing moment in the lives, one hopes, soon enough brought under the control of conscience, and not least, the social demands of a civilized society. Put differently, children old enough to go to school ought have learned to restrain that "seething cauldron," the Id—learned to set aside the imperious, lustful side of themselves in favor of a reasonably reliable civility. Actually, I have never heard children, even those rather disturbed psychologically, begin to equal in their wildest leaps of imagination, what now gets by as permissible for open distribution to newsstand purchasers or moviegoers. It is supposedly a privilege of our advanced state of civilization in the United States that magazines and books and filmstrips offering every imaginable kind of perversity are to be found in abundance everywhere.

I am often asked, as a child psychiatrist, what this terrible state of affairs means for our country's boys and girls, who have this recent social condition as an inheritance. In Stoughton many of the picketers gave their children as the source of motivation—a sincere desire to protect them from a local infestation of pornography. I don't at all deny the threat to children of pornography. But children can't be "protected" morally and spiritually by the closing down of one, two, even a thousand pornographic stores. Pornography reaches into our very midst: our homes, where the television sets universally are; the magazine racks in our neighborhood businesses; the supposedly acceptable theaters, where we go to see the latest films, not rarely full of sex employed to cheapen all of us—the scriptwriter, the actor or actress, the producer and director, and not least, the viewer.

How are we to protect our children from an *entire culture* become in so many instances vulgar—obsessively, coyly, or blatantly pornographic? I have no grand answers, but I hope that store in Stoughton, Massachusetts, is put out of business by those aroused mothers and fathers, and I surely wish the same goes for *Hustler* and *Penthouse* and dozens of magazines like them, and I wish our television programs and movies were not saturated with the coarse and the gross—and yes, I wish our minds and hearts would consider, yet again and with alarm, whether millions and millions of us have to keep putting up with a pornography that seems ever escalating in its impact on American family life.

December 1983

On Women's Liberation

My wife and I have spent over two decades talking with American families of various kinds, and we've certainly seen some awful instances of injustice connected with gender difference. We have seen women work long and hard for meager wages—often doing the same work as men, but paid substantially less. We have seen all sorts of discrimination, prejudice, and plain mean-spiritedness inform the way employers and, sad to say, husbands and fathers have treated women—to use W. H. Auden's phrase, "a whole climate of opinion": women belong here, are suited only for this, shouldn't be allowed to go there or do that. Is there really any argument any more over the economic disparities, the educational restrictions and inequities that have been the burden of America's women—among others elsewhere in the world—for so very long? In my medical school class there were four women; now, in the medical school classes I teach, there are dozens and dozens of women, and they are fine students, and make decent, caring physicians. So it has gone in other professions—from severe limitations, if not outright exclusion, to a gradual and (of late) more vigorous spirit of acceptance.

The issue now is not (one hopes and prays) whether women "deserve" equal pay for equal work, or "deserve" entry into the professions or access to jobs in companies or institutions once unwelcoming. The issue now is a much broader, cultural one: the so-called "role" of women in this life, and just as important, the "role" of men as well. Here we come to a highly complicated matter which has people of honorable intention at serious odds (I need not mention the demagogues on both sides). For it is hard to know how much of our "nature" as individuals has to do with our biological make-up, and how much is a consequence of our experiences, including the early years of childhood. This "nature-nurture" polarity will perhaps never lend itself to mathematical formulation—but it does seem foolish to exclude *either* of those two broad aspects of influence, and it does seem that some individuals and groups tend to side in almost a creedal fashion with one or the other: our inherited constitutional disposition as against our accumulation of learned expectations.

Of course, even the explicitly psychological qualities children learn at home and school and in the neighborhood are often a source of additional polarization, as my wife and I have come to realize again and again in the course of our work: children are taught, at different times, to be tough, fiercely competitive, highly acquisitive, "hard as nails," insistently active, and assertively outgoing—and also to be gentle, companionable, friendly, caring, warmly sensitive, quiet and tactful and patient and generously giving. Many of the above qualities have become sorted out, in the minds of millions of us, as connected to sexuality—masculine in nature, feminine in nature. And yet, in many of us these traits in various combinations (and sometimes uneasily, or in outright conflict) manage to exist side by side.

The controversy comes when each of us declares our sense of how those various qualities (which are at once psychological and spiritual) ought be *encouraged* to sort themselves out—what relative balance in which people. Oh, to be sure, one can say: the same ideal mix, never to be perfectly realized, is what everyone should seek. Yet, no society is without a division of labor. Even in utopian communes different people have chosen or been asked to do different deeds. As for the Bible (both the Old and New Testaments), it offers plenty of evidence of angry, war-like postures and utterly tranquil and accepting postures, of toughness in the name of God and of mild acquiescence in the name of God. Jesus could be as kindly and embracing as the human mind can imagine, and He could be demanding, argumentative, irritated, ready to take on His opponents. As for our babies, our growing children, I don't think there is too much disagreement about their *various* requirements: at different times in their lives they are in need of receiving a wide range of encouragement from their parents and others, who must show them how to love (by the example of being loved, needless to say), and how to be kindly and thoughtful—but also how to stand up for themselves and take care of themselves and learn a certain forceful independence and assertive individuality of spirit.

But who will be offering what qualities to whom—and with what kind of social and cultural sanction? Are women "liberated" when they, finally, not only become well paid executives and lawyers, but also become as eagerly truculent as their male colleagues in this law firm, that business—and live a life very much like their counterparts who are men: up early, to work, home late, then more work? As for children, are women also "liberated" when they cease wanting them, or if they hand over without fear and trembling their infant sons and daughters to day care centers, to nannies or to a succession of hired helpers, or yes, to husbands/fathers? I suppose, in view of the last mentioned alternative, I ought to ask this question: are men "liberated" when they learn to emphasize their affectionate responses to children, and to the natural world around them, and so doing, lose interest in the only jobs available to them, or even all jobs—preferring to stay home and care for their children?

These are vexing questions, and I don't pretend to have the answers to them. I do know that women of so-called working-class background have kept telling my wife and me that they work because they must, to stay afloat financially—that they would very much prefer to stay at home, be with their children. I do know that the men we've met who are anxious to initiate *their* "liberation" do not live in "factory towns," are not blue collar or white collar workers—but quite well educated individuals with all sorts of possibilities open to them. Often they can work at home as well as be a father who takes care of his children. The issue, rather commonly, is one of class—who, of what background, wants to be (and can afford to be) what kind of person, living what kind of life.

But I believe the issue, finally, becomes a moral one—and yes, one of renunciation as well as further "fulfillment." These days in America the latter is on so many of our minds—how to get more, be more. Women don't have this, men don't have that—well, let's all be "liberated," meaning we're as free now to acquire more and more attributes, experiences, opportunities, advantages. But how well can anyone do just about everything? There are only so many possibilities for attempted perfection, so to speak: as in the workplace, one learns by doing, and in this case, by *being*—and that means, being a mother, being a father, or alternatively, not being one or the other. Where in the world did we get the notion that it is our destiny to master all "roles," be all things to each other, including our growing children?

Does anyone really believe that young children are best sent to day care centers—as opposed to being brought up by a mother who gladly is there for them? For millions and millions of American families there is no way that a father can stay at home; and alas, it is harder and harder for mothers to stay home. As for the fathers who must work, they provide all sorts of moral and psychological gifts, not to mention the obvious financial ones, as the breadwinner: the example of hard work, of devotion to that work, of personal responsibility, of sacrifice on behalf of others, of dedication to a given series of personal obligations, of satisfaction in an achievement done, and done resolutely, continually. The working-class mothers my wife and I have interviewed do likewise—but almost universally (to repeat myself) yearn to be with their children instead of at work. Not so, of course, with the upper-middle class women we've interviewed.

I know no other way to put it: I believe that children need mothers and fathers both; that mothers are not fathers, and fathers are not mothers, nor ought the two be blurred into one—as in the dreary neuter word "parenting"; that it is wonderful for two individuals to complement one another, add to each other's store of possibilities—as inheritance for their children; and that the significance of the biological distinctions between men and women, amplified by centuries of religiously and culturally encouraged and sanctioned differences, are not to be altogether scorned, even as some of those differences must be gladly discarded, and even as individuals sort themselves out according to both their aspirations and responsibilities—and our world, one hope, becomes a more equitable place for all of us.

January–February 1984

On Homosexuality

This is another subject, like abortion, I find quite difficult to discuss: the matter of one's attitude toward homosexuality—i.e., one's moral and religious view with respect to the increasing phenomenon of a particular sexual orientation or inclination becoming the basis for social affirmations and political actions of various sorts. Like most psychiatrists, I've worked with young men and women who, out of nowhere it often seems to them, have found themselves to be "visited" (one patient put it) by a "condition," he called it, which he'd not chosen, and didn't know what to think of, morally, let alone (in the course of everyday life) live with or accept as a particular fate. Like most psychiatrists, too, I've learned that Freud was right to emphasize (as any number of novelists and poets have done before and after him) that just about all of us have (a matter of common sense, really) strong emotional involvements with both men and women (mothers and fathers, aunts and uncles, brothers and sisters, classmates of both sexes, and so on), and such involvements, like all human involvements, become highly charged, so to speak. Put differently, our affections are not at all confined to those of one sex, and in our minds (the back of them, and sometimes a bit near to the front) we feel in ourselves a strength of affection that may not be precisely sexual, but draws on the mind's, the body's sense of intimacy and devotion.

Freud was rather proper, his research interests notwithstanding. On social and cultural matters he was, actually, conservative. He was, really, a middle-class burgher in many ways. When he wrote of our "bisexuality," he did not mean what that word now has come to mean, namely an active sexuality that embraces both sexes. He simply (or not so simply!) means that as children we usually develop quite strong attachments to adults of both sexes, our mothers and fathers especially, and our brothers and sisters, and that those attachments are quite physical in nature, involve touching and hugging and kissing: stimulation of mind and body both. Such experiences have their own persistence, stay with us throughout life; albeit, in most of us, they get sorted out in such a way that our later attachments to the opposite sex are much strengthened versions (physically) of those earlier attachments, whereas our attachments to the same sex are—well, I guess the word is—"attenuated," or characterized by what Freud called the "sublimations" civilized people are wont to achieve: urgent and demanding passions stripped of their compelling energy, which get channeled elsewhere, that is, into the thoughts and deeds of decent, reflective, law-abiding citizens.

In some of us, however, it does not work like that—and for reasons I don't think (at least in many instances) any of us in my field really quite understand. Not that theories or all-too dogmatic, insistent explanations don't abound: genes, early childhood experiences (of course!), later traumas of various kinds, hormonal imbalances, severe losses and disappointments, the pressures of a given life which prompt reactions of various kinds, including sexual ones. In any event, every year thousands of young men and women find themselves aware, suddenly, or not so suddenly, of homosexual fantasies, dreams, impulses, desires, longings—find themselves, not rarely, deciding that they have a "problem" or "conflict" in that regard, or that they "are" homosexual, and that is that. Psychiatrists see an uncertain percentage of such men and women. It is my hunch that we are seeing fewer rather than more homosexually inclined youths—probably because there is, without question, less social stigmatization at stake and, consequently, less so-called "secondary anxiety," based on the fear of what would happen if the person in question acted upon his or her sexual desires. Moreover, many of us psychiatrists have in the past had our own kind of zealotry—our decision to call homosexuals not only "troubled" (and aren't we all, in one way or another!), but sick, sick, sick. In fact, of course, there is a not so pleasing (to some people, at least) egalitarianism in Freudian theory: *everyone* is "neurotic" in one fashion or another (according to that theory) and we all are supposed to be holding on hard for dear (psychological) life, though admittedly, some of us are stronger, are more successful in so doing than others. A colleague of mine, in that tradition, says that everyone's mind is like Macy's basement: you can find just about anything in it, if you probe long and hard enough. A decent clinician, it seems to me, ought to be humble and considerate and respectful when it comes to the subject of homosexuality. Maybe that clinician would be (one hopes and prays) honest enough to reach out, to acknowledge life's mysteries, to try to help another of God's children, in whatever way possible, even as we all need a helping hand in one way or another.

I've gone on long enough (given the space alloted me here) on this matter from the angle of 20th-century psychoanalytic relativism, one might call it. There is, besides, the more urgent matter of 20th-century *social* and *moral* relativism—the increasing sense in our Western secular societies that differences between people are simply ordinary, expectable facts of life, and that we ought accept them not only without surprise or annoyance or self-righteousness, but with a certain prideful sense of sophistication and achievement: this is the late 20th century, and *here* is what we know, and *this* is how we've learned to live! Homosexuality as yet another "life style"!

How ought one in mind, heart, soul respond to that last kind of cultural development? How ought that question be answered by someone who tries to be mindful of Jesus as He walked ancient Palestine, attending the world's sinners, the rich and the poor, the lame, the blind, the scorned, the rebuked, the downcast and downtrodden, the imprisoned and condemned, whose company He'd soon enough join? How ought His manner of approaching humankind in all its variously flawed conditions persuade us to consider this vexing matter of homosexuality? One prays hard lest arrogance and smugness and meanness of heart overwhelm one's judgment— no small matters, given the snide comments, the persecutory violence (of word and deed, sometimes police sanctioned or implemented) visited upon homosexuals over the past decades.

I would say this as my way of seeing this matter: I do not see that I have the moral authority to condemn another person for his or her sexual makeup. I believe we all owe each other compassionate understanding. But I also believe we do not owe each other that ultimate condescension which takes the form of a refusal to acknowledge our obligation to make moral distinctions. My "understanding," even if untouched by the sin of pride and smallness of heart and mind, is not meant to include a toleration of violence, cruelty, hatefulness, obscene sexuality, no matter the sex of the participants. One makes various criticisms or condemnations as a duty—the obligations that go with one's membership in a given moral (and spiritual) community. I find abhorrent the contemporary *cultural* emphasis on homosexuality; I find it sad that a particular aspect of human behavior has become the basis of a political movement, a so-called "liberation" movement. For homosexuals there is something demeaning about subsuming their daily existence under such a confining rubric: "gays." The mind boggles at heterosexuals, in all their diversity, so narrowly defining themselves: "straights." Such diversity holds for homosexuals, too—"all sorts and conditions," as the Book of Common Prayer reminds us.

I recognize the past injustices directed at men and women who, after all, did not choose at birth how their sexuality would develop. Nor is it easy for me to approach this matter as one only of *will;* nor, for me, do epithets come to mind, or excited denunciations. This vexing issue does not require the attention of scolds. But I dislike the politicization of a personal matter; and the social and cultural words that have emerged under the word "gay" in various American cities are for me sad and regrettable developments, and in certain places, certain respects, thoroughly obnoxious to behold. "Let it all hang out," we heard in the 1960s from the "counterculture." Well, God save us! The absence of restraint, and yes, of guilt and shame (in connection with all sorts of lusts we have, heterosexual and homosexual, not to mention those connected to the worship of Mammon) means the loss of our distinctive humanity: the creature on this planet who uses language, thinks, reflects, and has been inspired by God to tame, not flaunt, the passions, use their energy in order to harness the world, so that we may all live a better life, and not least, so that we may wonder and pray about this life's meaning. We owe each other tact, discretion, the right of individuality—and a consideration of what kind of public values, what kind of larger social and cultural scene, we want for the world's children. I do not think the question of homosexuality as it now increasingly exists in this country ought be regarded without the foregoing consideration: the implications for a nation's sense of itself, what it sanctions or celebrates within itself as communities (as opposed to individual inclinations).

Moreover, a number of homosexuals have told me of their dismay at what gets called "gay liberation"—and their anger that any refusal to go along with a highly publicized mode of self-representation gets immediately denounced as cowardice or hypocrisy or selfishness: an instance of ideology, with its built-in protections, and ironically, an instance of moral and psychological condemnation not unlike that experience in the past by homosexuals at the hands of their various accusers. The point for these men and women is their privacy, their dignity, their struggle to live *on their own* an honorably decent life—without being hectored, yes, but also without becoming themselves hectors: members of yet another pushy, truculent, self-important pressure group in this grimly secular society.

March 1984

Impressions of Nicaragua—Part I

Recently I went with two of my sons to Nicaragua, where we spent time visiting schools (then in session), hospitals, clinics, a number of Managua's barrio homes, and those of other cities, such as Masaya and Leon. We visited relatively isolated campesino communities, talked with many boys and girls whose parents work long hours on the land. We also talked with nuns and priests, some of them Americans working gladly, enthusiastically in the country, others of Nicaraguan ancestry, and very much torn by conflicting loyalties, sentiments, aspirations. We came back to this country, I fear, as worried and confused as some of our Nicaraguan clergy friends quite obviously were.

Even some strong critics of the Sandinista government acknowledge its valuable educational and medical achievements. In the journal *Foreign Affairs* (Summer 1983), Arturo Cruz, who resigned his position as Nicaragua's Ambassador to the United States in protest against the increasingly totalitarian nature of his government, describes the Sandinistas as showing a "real concern for the destitute" (who, one has to add, make up the overwhelming majority of the nation's people). At another point Cruz refers to "programs worthy of praise," and characterizes them as "targeted at improving the living conditions of the Nicaraguan people." He mentions "a literacy campaign and a public health service reform designed to benefit the entire country." Toward the end of his essay he refers to the "idealistic boys and girls" who make up, by his estimate, "the Revolution's rank and file."

Such idealism seemed very much in evidence to us as we traveled through Nicaragua. The literacy program has been dramatically effective. Among those who helped in that effort were youths of the upper and middle classes in Managua who attended a Catholic

85

school, *Instituto Pedagogico—La Salle*. The principal of that school, Edwin Maradiaga, a native-born priest, was eloquent in his description of what took place in recent years:

> For our students this was the opportunity of their lives. They had lived in a protected world of their own. In this country under Somoza half the country had an income of less than 100 American dollars *a year*. The Somoza family alone owned a quarter of all our arable land. They and a handful of their cronies had total power and huge wealth, while 80 percent of the people had no water, and two thirds of them no electricity, and half no sanitary facilities at all, and nearly three quarters of all Nicaraguans lived in houses with dirt floors. Over 100 of every 1,000 children born died as infants. Malaria and tuberculosis and terrible gastroenteritis and typhoid were everywhere taking life. Those were diseases that could have been prevented. Now we are waging a major war on them, as with our literacy campaign.
>
> Our students have learned all these statistics. Once they didn't know them, because—to be frank—we didn't teach them. We didn't know them ourselves! It is not only the poor here whose lives are different! Many of our students—their fathers are business and professional men—have never forgotten the experience of going into the barrios and the small villages, and teaching children of their age how to read and write. One of our boys came up to me and asked why he'd never been told about how his own people live. I gather he'd asked that question of his parents, too. I think many of us have been shaking our heads about the past and trying to work for a better future. I know [he reads American magazines] that your people have been told about the children of our prominent families who want to leave because of the fear of military service or because they don't like it here. True! But I've read about how many of your own young people, whose parents had money, got out of the draft when you were fighting in Vietnam; and I wish someone would tell your people how many of our young people from very comfortable families have been given a real jolt of idealism by this Revolution!

He is a reflective priest, by no means willing to allow the above observations to take complete control of his mind. He knew that there are tough ideologues hard at work among the Sandinistas— anxious to give short shrift to the desire many have for a social democratic outcome. He was (he still is, I would imagine) in a terrible bind, not unlike that of Arturo Cruz (though the latter has chosen exile, and this priest must struggle every day for some minimal working relationship with Nicaragua's ruling clique). For Fr. Maradiaga history is a constant companion—memories of a terrible dictatorship, and an awareness that such a national experience doesn't simply go away when revolution succeeds in banishing, at long last, a man like Somoza and his corrupt and cruel associates. "We lived with fear and bitterness every day here, for over four decades, and we knew that the outside world, by and large, didn't care much that we were a country enslaved," he pointed out to us, my sons especially, who kept wondering how it was that a country they love, the United States of America, could be so indifferent for so long to the ordeal of Nicaragua under the Somoza family—and now be so vigorously sensitive to the mistakes and wrongdoing of the Sandinistas. We were being told by a gentle, forgiving, sensitive priest that evil once consolidated over time has its own persisting authority. We were also being reminded, tactfully but firmly, of the longstanding involvement between our Marines and Nicaragua's social and economic and political history. After decades of encampment in that country, the Marines handed power over to the Somoza family in the mid-1930s.

Still, past errors and sins do not justify new outbursts of self-righteous arrogance, never mind statist repression. Fr. Maradiaga was exhilarated by the idealism he had witnessed in recent years, but he had good reason to be concerned about the fate of his country—and not only because it has been under pressure from abroad. The Sandinistas, by their own admission, have made serious mistakes in their approach to the Miskito Indian population; have gathered unto themselves the exclusive reins of power; have curbed dissent; and yes, have shown themselves to be (in my opinion) uncritical of the sort of Marxist ideology that Cuba and its sponsor the Soviet Union press upon the Third World. Nor have Managua's *commandantes* shown any enormous sensitivity to the religious passions and yearnings in the Nicaraguan people or to the truly revolutionary possibilities such a Christian spirit offers—a matter (that of religion in Nicaragua today) I shall discuss in my next column.

April 1984

Impressions of Nicaragua—Part II

In the well-to-do sections of Managua, and other cities of Nicaragua, such as Masaya or Leon, the Pope's picture may be seen displayed proudly on the doors of houses, in any number of windows. In the stores frequented by business or professional people the same holds—the Pontiff's familiar smiling face is a constant presence. But in the barrios, and indeed, in the homes of campesinos, who work Nicaragua's land for sugar or cotton, one sees the Pope rarely, if at all. Jesus, yes—He is everywhere, even sometimes in the homes of quite radical Sandinista people. But the Pope for a good number of Nicaraguans loyal to the present government has become controversial, to say the least.

I asked one woman who lived in a Managua barrio to help me understand why I saw no picture of John Paul II anywhere in that community, yet so many pictures of him in the homes (many quite elegant) near the Inter-Continental Hotel, the fancy place where my ilk stays, at least in the first days of a visit to the country. This woman was not especially political—as were several others I met, who were so-called "block leaders," hence tied to the government's power, and yes, its largesse (the control of sugar or flour distribution). She was, really, an ordinary person who for years had worked in a small factory as a seamstress. She had known her fair share of suffering and tragedy, and yet had somehow managed to keep her spirits reasonably high—and also to keep her faith. When we began talking about the Pope, I noticed that she lowered her head immediately, and paused for a longer spell than had ever before been her custom. She seemed almost to inhale deeply before she started making her statement:

I do not think the Holy Father's visit here was a good one! We

88

wanted to see him. He is our shepherd. But he became [the cause of] a big argument. When I saw him being booed, I was upset. Then I heard our government's side, and I was upset again. I kept wondering why the Pope let this happen. I think he doesn't like our government. He may be right in some of his criticism, but no Pope ever came here and gave a lecture to the Somozas, during all the years they ruled us; and when we would ask the priests why the Church doesn't stand up to the Somozas, we were told that the Church doesn't mix in politics. But now the Pope does. It's all too much for me to figure out!

That last moment of avowed intellectual incapacity soon enough gives way to a somewhat agitated series of assertions, interposed with pleas for God's mercy:

We were brought up to worship Jesus and be glad Somoza is our boss. That's what every important person said; and if your children went to Catholic schools, they heard that there, too. My sister has been a maid to a lawyer's family, and so she has heard everything! Now we have a new government, and the lawyer is unhappy, and suddenly the Pope is his hero. Good! I only hope that lawyer follows the Pope all the way! I only wish the Pope would get the rich people of the world together and give them a tough lecture, the way he did our government. Maybe we're making mistakes, like you said, and like your country says, but this is new—how everyone wants to make us so perfect! May God save not only us, but the people who want us to stop making mistakes. May God help us see better. May God save us from your Marines.

Do those Marines know why Nicaragua is suddenly a big enemy of theirs? Maybe some of our *commandantes* have stumbled, but why are the North Americans so scared? They lived happily with our Somoza. Now we're one of their biggest enemies. Even my sister's boss thinks it's a "bad joke." He told her that "the North Americans see shadows everywhere, because they have so much money, and they're always afraid someone is hiding and will take something away from them." I wish the Pope would go to Washington and lecture people there, the way he did here. May God bless the Holy Father!

Again and again I heard people such as her express their loyalty to the Catholic Church, their sadness at the increasing tension between the Church and the Sandinista government, their memory of a Church once all too acquiescent to the Somozas, their memory, too, of a Church increasingly at odds with the Somozas toward the end of their tyrannical rule. Among many well-to-do people, on the other hand, the Church has become a rallying ground of sorts:

> It's the one time I feel free, these days—when I go to Mass. I pray to God that He will intervene, and save us from Communism. This country is now run by a dictatorship, and the only institution that is left to say no to those *commandantes* is our Church. They would destroy the Church in a minute, if they thought they could get away with it. They organized that mob that heckled the Pope. They are trying to set up their own puppet-Church. But the people won't be so docile. The people want to believe in God, not Castro and Ortega and the local political henchman with his slogans. The people are tired of these new bosses. Many of us who fought the Somozas are now being called Devils, Somocistas—by these Sandinistas, who claim the sole power, the sole truth. No wonder they don't want the Church strong: they don't want to kneel before God—only before their own political beliefs.

The themes these speakers bring up are not new in 20th-century history: a compromised Church, an arrogant secularism. In Nicaragua my sons and I saw extraordinary American nuns and priests, working hard and long on behalf of the country's poor. We also met inspiring priests and nuns, doing likewise, who were born in the country, and were struggling to reconcile their enthusiasm for various social changes wrought by the government with their awareness of the chill (to put it mildly) between their Church's hierarchy and their nation's leaders. We met priests and parishioners alarmed and disgusted by what they regarded as a totalitarian regime, determined to take command of their country's economic, political, cultural—and yes, religious life. We met priests and parishioners who saw mistakes being made, but who also professed great loyalty, still, to the Sandinista government (especially so, as it came under increasing assault from the American-backed Somocista-riddled "contras") and great loyalty, still, to the Catholic Church. One priest put matters a bit bluntly to me:

> If I argue with the Pope about his view of our government, your countrymen become alarmed. They say I'm becoming a heretic, a dupe of the Communists. But look at your American Catholic

Church—the way you North Americans disobey the Pope again and again. When he lectures you, criticizes you—well, you smile and pat him on the back and say you love him, then go back to your contraceptives and abortions and greedy materialism and divorces and MX missiles, despite his encyclicals against your whole way of living and your selfishness. Do the Americans who are glad to see the Pope become a symbol of faith for those fighting against the Sandinistas ever take the time to read the Pope's remarks on capitalism, and on militarism and nuclear warfare?

After that rhetorical question was put, the padre looked at the cross on his study's wall, and prayed—"for your country, for mine." He prayed also "for the Sandinista revolution" and "for all revolutions"—prayed not that they without criticism achieve one or another stated goal, but that something else happen: "I beg that our revolution becomes a Christian revolution. I beg that Christ's radical and gentle spirit, both, touch our people and their leaders—and your people and your leaders."

May 1984

Psychology as Faith

At various moments in these columns I have made snide references to the secular idolatry which it has been the fate of psychology and psychiatry to become for so many of us. My wife and our sons have suggested I spell out some of my thoughts on this subject, hence this essay. I must say that I speak as one of the gullible, the susceptible, the all too readily devotional—having put in years of teaching in medicine and pediatrics, in psychiatry and child psychiatry, in psychoanalysis, and done so with an eagerness and zeal and self-assurance, if not self-importance, I have yet to shake off, no matter these words, and others I'll write before I go to meet my Maker. "Once smitten, for life smitten," as a teacher of mine in high school used to say, and how we mocked his arrogant determinism, we who were so sure that no one or nothing would get its teeth into us unless we rationally and with utterly independent judgment had decided that such be the case.

In fact, I think we need to know why that teacher's observation does so commonly turn out to be true—the intellectual and psychological, and not least, social and economic "investment," so to speak, we make in what amounts to a way of thinking, as well as a career. The issue, as always, is pride, the sin of sins. To be a psychiatrist in America today, one says with all the risks of even more pride, of narcissism, is to take a substantial risk with one's spiritual future, as Anna Freud obliquely declared in one of her books *(Normality and Pathology in Childhood)*. There she rendered a chronicle of the unblinking credulity accorded any and every psychoanalytic assumption, however tentatively posited; and as she said more bluntly to a few of us at Yale Medical School in a meeting both instructive and unsettling during the mid-1970s: "I do not understand why so many people want us to tell them the answers to everything that happens in life! We have enough trouble figuring out the few riddles we are equipped to investigate!"

Well, of course, she *did* understand only too well what has happened, especially in America: the mind as a constant preoccupation for many people who are basically agnostic, and who regard themselves as the ultimate, if passing, reality—which preoccupation constitutes a socially and historically conditioned boost to the egoism or narcissism we all must confront in ourselves. The result is everywhere apparent: parents who don't dare bring up their children, from infancy on, without recourse to one expert's book, then another's; students who are mesmerized by talk of psychological "stages" and "phases" and "behavioral patterns" and "complexes"; grown-up people who constantly talk of an "identity crisis" or a "mid-life crisis"; elderly men and women who worry about "the emotional aspects of old age," and those attending them at home or in the hospital who aim at becoming versed in steering the "dying" through *their* "stages" or "phases"; newspaper columnists, if not gurus, and their counterparts on television who have something to say about every single human predicament—the bottom line being, always, a consultation with a "therapist"; and worst of all, the everyday language of our given culture, saturated with psychological expressions, if not banalities, to the point that a Woody Allen movie strikes one not as exaggeration, caricature, or satire, but as documentary realism.

Especially sad and disedifying is the preoccupation of all too many clergy with the dubious blandishments of contemporary psychology and psychiatry. I do not mean to say there is no value in understanding what psychoanalytic studies, and others done in this century by medical and psychological investigators, have to offer any of us who spend time with our fellow human beings—in the home, in school, at work, and certainly, in the various places visited by ministers and priests. The issue is the further step not a few of today's clergy have taken—whereby "pastoral counseling," for instance, becomes their major ideological absorption and the use of the language of psychology their major source of self-satisfaction. Surely we are in danger of losing our religious faith when the chief satisfaction of our lives consists of an endless attribution of psychological nomenclature to all who happen to come our way.

I am tired, for instance, of the unwarranted, undeserved acquiescence some ministers (and alas, recently, priests as well) show to various "experts" who tell them about important "relationships" (talking about psychological jargon) and about "mental health" (whatever *that* is) and about the supposed "value" of religion (the height of condescension) in a person's so-called "psychic economy." I am tired of watching ministers or priests mouth psychiatric pieties, when "hard praying" (as I used to hear it put in the rural South) is what the particular human being may want, and yes, urgently require. I am tired of all the "value-free" declarations in the name of what is called "social science"; tired, too, of the complexities, ambiguities, and paradoxes of our moral life being swept into yet another "developmental scheme," with "stages" geared to ages.

As Walker Percy reminded us, and we ought keep reminding ourselves, one can "get all A's and flunk life"—meaning one can answer some psychological theorist's hypothetical moral scenarios brilliantly in a given office or research setting, and then go into this world of sin and drive a car like an arrogant murderer, or push ahead in dozens of other ways that any moment may provide.

Back in the 1930s a host of brilliant people, including psychiatrists, psychologists, physicians, and alas, philosophers, ministers, and priests made their various accommodations, if not scandalous agreements of support, with the Nazis. Those highly educated ones might have scored well in some psychological theorist's "scale" of moral development; might have obtained good results in a Rorschach test, in a TAT test; might have mastered the Minnesota Multi-Phasic examinations; might have gotten top scores in our SAT tests given prospective college students; might have been pronounced in possession of "stable personalities" by an examining psychiatrist—all too "stable," they were, all too in resonance with that much touted "reality principle," namely Hitler's murderous authority.

Dietrich Bonhoeffer was a singular person indeed, and when he blasted psychology and psychiatry, as he did in his prison letters, we ought take sharp notice. (We ought take sharp notice, too, of efforts to stifle criticism of aspects of psychology or psychiatry. When such criticism gets called "resistance," or a mark of a "problem"—then an ideology is at work: agree with us or be banished!) Bonhoeffer, it seems, was prophetic not only with respect to his nation's tragedy in the 1930s and early 1940s, but also with respect to the continuing threats which certain aspects of 20th-century Western thinking pose to people of religious faith.

June 1984

Teen-Age Pregnancy:
A Moral Matter

We hear constantly, these days, of the surging rate of teen-age pregnancies, and we hear, too, what ought to be done to stop a phenomenon often called an "epidemic." Thousands and thousands of young, unmarried women of high school age, and even junior high school age, become pregnant at a time when they are just beginning to grow up physically and mentally—only now to face the awesome responsibility of bearing within themselves someone else's early life.

As this national tragedy has worsened, the responses of certain segments of our pluralist society have been interesting indeed. One hears that the problem is mainly medical: a matter of increased and more effective use of contraceptives, and in the event of a pregnancy, a prompt abortion. So-called "sex education" courses are what one hears constantly recommended in this quarter: teach those youths "preventive hygiene," I've heard it called, meaning specific "techniques" to make pregnancy unlikely. As for those instances where the various devices or procedures have somehow failed, an abortion clinic will quickly solve the "problem." A large number of our country's abortions are today being done on adolescents—and upon no small number of them, two abortions have been performed.

I am dismayed by what I hear, in this regard, from significant numbers of the well educated, liberal intelligentsia, medical and nonmedical alike. Again and again I hear "educational" aspects of the problem discussed, or, of course, the "psychological" side of things. My medical colleagues, all too many of them, tell me that "those girls" (it is mostly put) or "those women" are "immature,"

95

are "ignorant of birth control information," are "acting out" serious psychological difficulties, hence are in dire need of "help." Even some of my friends who oppose abortion on religious principle shake their heads in sorrow that a given woman, still a child in many ways, has come to such a pass—and wish that she had "known enough" to avoid her predicament, or will receive enough "counseling" to avoid another such occurrence.

"Meanwhile," as one doctor recently said to me about a patient of his, "we must now do an abortion." That particular girl in question actually didn't herself want an abortion. She very much wanted the child she was bearing. She had grown up alone, sad, constantly anxious. Her parents had separated when she was a baby. Her mother was a difficult, demanding, and at times brutally punitive person. Her father had served time in jail for armed robbery, and was mean and cold—described by prison doctors as a "psychopath." I remember talking with her and hearing this: "All I want is a baby; then I can forget the rest of the world, and try to be nice to her, and make up for what I missed." There was more, a good deal more, but I doubt a million additional words of hers would have added much to those above—a summary statement of a kind I've heard from so many teen-age women who are pregnant.

They are often hurt, moody, terribly vulnerable, shut off emotionally from just about everyone, especially their parents—and the prospect of having a baby (usually imagined to be a girl) seems welcome, to say the least. "This baby will be a gift of God to me," one young lady of 15 told me. I asked her how she had come to that conclusion, and her response was unforgettably poignant: "There is no one in the world who cares about me, only God, and I feel Him looking at me sometimes, and He must have felt sorry for me, so He sent this baby to me."

I wouldn't even want to speculate (at least in this limited space) upon the psychological, not to mention theological, implications of her statement—this impoverished, battered child of 15 who so desperately desired to find herself, and yes, her God, in a pregnancy. But I remember the welfare worker's annoyance—that a truant from school had missed her "sex education" classes. I remember the doctor's annoyance—that yet another ghetto youth, as he put it, was "on her way." I asked him the direction of that "way," and heard this: "One pregnancy after another." A bit further in our conversation he, too, summoned "sex education" as the "answer," and, as well, contraceptives, abortions. With respect to the last, he was emphatic. "What are we to do, let these kids drown in their own children? They are children themselves. They can't even take care of themselves, never mind one baby, never mind four or five more." As for the adamant wish of this particular "child" for a baby, surely both of us as doctors could recognize the "psychopathology" at work.

I fear that what I recognize at work among so many of us who worry about this vexing issue is quite something else—a condescension, a failure of spiritual nerve, which have us patronizing many young women, if not consigning them to the ranks of a moral *Lumpenproletariat*. We offer them contraceptives—meaning a sexuality without pregnancy, and meaning a continuation of their desperate and often futile search for someone who will respect them and help them redeem themselves as the particular human beings they are. We offer them "sex education," and a smattering of psychological talk—to a similar effect. We offer them, finally, abortion—meaning that to *their* "death at an early age" we are willing to add an even earlier termination of life.

How might we, alternatively, approach this matter? We treat symptoms, not causes, when we offer biology lessons and psychological jargon and pills and jellies and, God forbid, abortions to young women who are (they will say so over and over again) lost, bewildered, desperately hungry—sometimes literally so, but always spiritually so: for a sense of purpose and meaning in life, for something (for someone) to believe in, for moral direction, not to be confused with sexual "techniques," contraceptive gadgets, medical procedures.

Our cosmopolitan newspaper editorialists and all those medical and psychological authorities who have become big-deal secular gods want these women out of the way: stop having those babies, learn how to "plan parenthood," and we in our comfortable self-importance can turn to another "issue." In contrast, Jesus offered great and humble love to such women—saw in their pain and loneliness His own.

Where is the spiritual energy of our privileged young, and of our professional men and women—people who might offer to share themselves with these needy "others," these fellow human beings? The redemption Dostoyevsky portrays in *Crime and Punishment* is Christian, mediated through human spiritual love; and similarly for

Malcolm X, another "hopeless criminal" who wondrously was "transformed."

Once in a ghetto of Atlanta I heard a young woman plead for "someone to talk to." She needed "counseling," we all thought. But she added this: "Someone to talk to, so I'll be able to find myself, and know what I believe, and what I mustn't do, because it's wrong." She said "wrong"—not "costly," not "unnecessary," not "medically harmful," not "avoidable."

July–August 1984

On Sin

During my psychiatric residency I was supervised by a psycho-analyst who had a special interest in (and knowledge of) the phenomenon of guilt. She had her own way of listening to my reports of what I'd heard patients say; and invariably she'd remind me that there was "a problem of guilt" for one or another person I was seeing in psychotherapy.

I remember a particular patient, a woman of 25, a graduate student in literature, who made it hard for me to follow my supervisor's advice in interpreting the "guilty feelings" that (we both thought) were responsible for a given spell of depression. Every time I tried to come up with a clarification or interpretation, I was told by my patient that I didn't quite understand—that she was *ashamed* of herself, because she'd done something she knew to be wrong, whereas I was always talking to her about the guilt she felt, meaning an irrational or unconscious response on her part.

At the time I wasn't prepared to pay much attention to that most interesting distinction. My education and mode of thinking had persuaded me that we have all sorts of lusts and rages at work in the back of our minds, unbeknown to ourselves, and that we also experience a sense of wrongdoing within ourselves (also, rather often, unbeknown to ourselves) for having had such desires or such angry, even murderous surges of feeling.

Nor would I, today, doubt that the mind is, indeed, plagued by irrational and unconscious drives, which (in turn) are condemned by our consciences, often without our even knowing that such an arraignment or judgment has been made. What is interesting about our age is that we dwell so intently on such matters—as if the only kind of remorse we really know is unconscious, and is a response not to crimes of commission or even omission, but rather, of the imagination.

99

When I told my supervisor that my patient kept harkening back to a specific misdeed she had committed (a sexual liaison with her employer) I was reminded in no uncertain terms that such a stated source of discomfort was merely a "symbol" of "something deeper"—and what troubled the patient was the "unconscious significance" of the affair she'd had, meaning a guilt based on the connection her mind made between that boss, a 40-year-old store owner, and her father, who owned a good deal of property.

I mention the above with no conviction that any reader will be especially surprised by such a line of reasoning. The rhetoric of our everyday lives is saturated with the commonplaces of contemporary psychology. Yet, I believe I was instructed, over the long run, as much by that patient as by that supervisor. The patient remained adamant in her belief that a moral reckoning was required as much as a "catharsis"—a psychological foray into her mind's interior, with an attendant reprieve from her moodiness. One afternoon, in a sparely furnished room of a hospital's psychiatric clinic she offered this distinction to me—one I tried to forget but couldn't: "You keep trying to find the cause of my difficulty within me; but I believe there's someone else who has to be mentioned."

I looked intently at her, and waited in silence for her explanation. She said nothing. I wondered whom she had in mind—her mother, her father, her boyfriend, her brother, who was a rather self-righteous graduate student in philosophy. Still, silence—and so I spoke: "Did you have anyone particular you wanted to mention?" She gave me a thin smile, and proceeded to answer me indirectly—perhaps fearing that if she'd said, tersely, "God," I might have questioned her over-all sanity! What I heard from her went like this: she didn't doubt that there were psychological problems for her to solve, but she was struggling with the largest possible psychological problem, and I seemed unaware of it—what to think of her "transgression." Upon hearing that word used I immediately took careful notice out loud, as is the custom of my ilk, by looking intently at the speaker, raising an eyebrow, repeating the charged word, "transgression," with a portentous, questioning lift in the voice.

I needed a clarification and got it: "It is sin I'm talking about." I recall scratching my head, being puzzled. I remember asking this intelligent, forthright, brooding young lady what "sin" had to do with her worries, her fears, her downcast moods, which in their sum threatened to overcome her. I remember thinking to myself that she was, perhaps, sicker than I'd first realized, that (at the least) she was using a religious term to avoid discussing some quite serious and painful psychological matters. Her response to me was brief, pointed, firmly stated: "God's judgment matters more than my own."

Thereupon I lost control a bit—not in the sense of becoming agitated or even upset. I allowed myself to converse with her on her own territory. I entered into a complex theological discussion with her—trying to indicate to her that God surely did not intend for her to use Him as a means of repeated (and seemingly endless) self-laceration; that He would want her, rather, to forgive herself, as He had forgiven, in a way, all of us—redeemed our lives through His suffering. Nothing original in such observations—but the mere fact that they were being made represented a dramatic shift in a particular (clinical) acquaintance.

Soon enough I was the one who was perplexed, if not troubled: what to tell my supervisor? When I broached the subject in the weekly "supervisory session," began to indicate what had happened, got as far as the patient's declaration about "God's judgment," I encountered a stern, reproving look, then a comment as intuitive as it was didactic and demanding: "I hope you stayed clear of theology."

Nervous, fearful, quick to conclude I'd failed, eager to avoid direct criticism (talking about "judgments," God's and those we make upon one another!) I nodded agreement, said nothing about what I'd discussed with the patient of a religious nature, changed the tack of my presentation to my supervisor by offering her some new information I'd gleaned about the woman's childhood. I had not quite lied—or rather, I lied by intention rather than fact. And I felt sinful afterward—not guilty; sinful because I didn't have the courage and integrity to tell my supervisor, tell myself, how helpful it had been for that patient, for me as well, to have the discussion we'd had, to think about (assisted by another person) what is right and wrong in the largest moral perspective possible.

September 1984

On Grace

I remember a conversation with Erik Erikson back in the late 1960s. He was himself remembering a conversation with some psychoanalytic colleagues. The subject was Gandhi, his method of taking on the British, his way of living a life. Erikson had spent years trying to understand the Mahatma (the result was *Gandhi's Truth*), and in so doing had come to realize how difficult it is to "explain" psychologically the astonishing moral vitality of such a person.

As he tried to do just that, tell a few psychoanalysts what qualities of mind made for a particular leader, he found himself using the word "grace" again and again. Eventually he was challenged. What did he *mean* by that word "grace"? How would he *define* it? What explains its appearance in one or another person? "I told them," Erikson told me, "that I didn't know how to answer their questions—that if you are in the presence of grace, you sure know it, and you sure feel grateful."

His listeners, he knew, were not satisfied. Nor is it fair to accuse that handful of psychiatric specialists of being especially obtuse, wrongheaded, or narrowly reductionist. These days so many of us look to the social sciences for a definitive truth—and any assertion about this life that doesn't pass their muster (doesn't fit into some sociologist's or psychiatrist's scheme of things) is rather quickly viewed with skepticism if not suspicion, or indeed, outright contempt. Words such as "grace" are a relic (aren't they?) of another (pre-scientific) age, when men and women didn't understand the way the mind works, the way society comes to bear on the individual.

I struggle with such a mentality all the time—draw upon its

102

valuable side with gratitude, but stumble badly, all too often, because I fail to realize certain limits to a given way of seeing the world. Erikson knew that at a certain point Gandhi was much more than a collection of drives, impulses, reflexes finding their expression in a day-to-day life. For all his problems, for all his obvious limitations as a husband and a father, Gandhi had an important moral vision, and was willing to labor day and night for its realization. How to explain the emergence of such a vision, the energy put into the struggle for India's freedom? How to explain the transformation of a relatively privileged dandy into a man who was at pains to live a modest and simple life—in hopes, surely, of persuading other well educated and well-off Indians to follow suit?

Without question there are, indeed, psychological explanations for all human behavior, including that of Gandhi, or Dr. Albert Schweitzer, two well-known moral figures of the earlier decades of this century. No doubt both of them, and others whose virtuous lives we admire, were taught early on to be good and decent by parents who were themselves good and decent.

Still, anyone who has worked in a psychiatric clinic (and maybe a few people whose everyday experiences have given them a modest but important wisdom) knows that irony abounds in this world. Many parents try hard to teach their children proper values, only to find those sons or daughters not especially kind or considerate to others. Nor is it altogether impossible that a child who has been treated roughly, whose parents are mean or callous, will emerge relatively thoughtful and compassionate. Of course some parents who are honorable bring up honorable children, and some parents who are thoroughly dishonorable perpetuate their dismal qualities in their offspring.

I mention such psychological complexities and ambiguities because, really, they make any generalization grounded in the social sciences not sufficiently persuasive—an inadequate basis for explaining why people end up living as they do. One person's "masochism" is another person's patient willingness to work with and help the world's vulnerable and needy people. One person's "phobic personality" is another person's persisting realization that this planet is in constant jeopardy, given the many threats to our land, water, and atmosphere, not to mention the threats posed by our so-called "advanced" nations with their military hardware. One person's alcoholic despair is another person's capacity to use some whiskey as a help in escaping the constraints of ordinary thinking and living—to leap into a visionary trance of sorts in response to a particular moral stimulus.

Here is what I once heard Dorothy Day say: "As I serve them soup [the homeless poor, often alcoholic ones of New York City's Bowery] I often wonder why God meant for them to be them and me to be me. Visitors will sometimes ask me how I can 'take it'—and then I know what to say: that those visitors should ask some of our guests how *they* can 'take it,' putting up with us! I'm not being facetious! We are all children of God, and who knows but that the only difference between us is due to His grace, and therefore the mystery of our differences will never be solved until He gives us His reasons! There are days when I see our poor people being nicer to each other than some of us are, in this community, to each other—and then I realize that to judge a person or explain a person is the riskiest thing to do, as in 'Judge not lest ye be judged.'"

What does distinguish us is our behavior—how we act with and toward one another. Whatever our motives, problems, conflicts, our secret and not so secret passions, the real moral test of our worth has to be what we do with ourselves in the course of our everyday lives. No wonder Dorothy Day knew to avoid the all too satisfying distinctions of the definitely saved and the obviously damned. In a moment, she knew, any of us can slip into sin, and yes, any of us can find a redeeming moment's moral affirmation: God's grace which suddenly befalls us, enabling us to be more than we had any right to expect, more than any psychological or sociological theorist can ever explain on the basis of traits, influences, background.

Stumbling along we suddenly catch our stride, or running confidently we suddenly fall down—and maybe sometimes the "reason" is not in ourselves but in the stars, God's stars: His grace.

October 1984

Idealism

During the early 1960s I often heard the concerns of Southern civil rights activists as they contemplated one or another assault on segregationist power. They wanted and needed recruits—black and white youths able and willing to take the risks of police brutality, even imprisonment—and they sought those recruits actively on campuses within and outside the region.

Yet, sometimes there were second thoughts, as given voice in this instance by a black man of 24 who had been working in the "movement" for several years: "I don't know these white college kids. I've lived all my life here in the South, and most of them come from the North. They're from New England and New York; they're from Chicago and St. Louis and Cleveland; and they're from the West Coast. They're strangers to Alabama and Georgia and Mississippi. Lots of them have been to Europe once or twice, but never here. They want to help us out, and that's great. But every once in a while I take a look at them and wonder who they really are, and what's pushed them to us—to come down to our Dixie and tell us they want to help, and they know they might get hurt, hurt bad, even risk getting killed.

"I know the answer. They're good people. They want to change the world. They're idealists. I guess I should let the matter drop, right there. I shouldn't be suspicious. I should be grateful. But I still can't help wondering about them. Maybe it's because they're white and I'm a Southern 'colored boy'—when I'm not a 'nigger'! Maybe it's me—never trusting any white man, no matter who he is. And that brings up something else—the white *women* who come here: I'm even more suspicious of them. I just can't help it! I wasn't brought up to see white women be so comfortable with Negro people, especially Negro men—comfortable on an equal basis, not comfortable in ordering us around. I wasn't brought up to see white folks ready to help us, and share our troubles. I guess I don't have as much faith in human nature as I thought I did! I guess I've become cynical—or have never had any reason not to be cynical. These days I look at these white folks down here to help us, and I say to myself that they seem as good and unselfish and helpful as you could ever want—and then I catch myself wondering if they don't have something up their sleeves. You could say I'm wondering what their motives are. What's the phrase—'ulterior motives'? Then I feel ashamed of myself—when one of them comes in beaten up by a sheriff's stick!"

Around that time he wasn't the only one wondering why some people take action on behalf of others. The Peace Corps had recently been founded; Vista was in the works, a domestic program aimed at directing the good will of certain eager youths to the serious problems of the poor. Again and again government officials were trying to figure out what kind of people ought be accepted in these programs—how to sort out the solidly idealistic ones from those who would end up a source of trouble to themselves or to those others meant to be helped. I remember, for instance, social science colleagues of mine going to Washington, attending conferences, assembling their various "profiles" and "criteria," their characterizations of various "personality types"—a means of determining the "mental health" of various "applicants."

I remember my own work with SCLC (Southern Christian Leadership Conference) and SNCC (Student Nonviolent Coordinating Committee), those mainstays of activism in the South of, say, 1963 and 1964. I remember the "orientation session" we had, 20 years ago, in Oxford, Ohio, a prelude to the Mississippi Summer Project of 1964—to which hundreds of Northern college students eagerly flocked. During that spell of preparation for the trek Southward, I was repeatedly asked to consider *this* youth, and then *that* youth: what did I think of his or her purposes, soundness of mind, ability to take the stresses ahead, overall good judgment, capacity to work well with others?

Such questions often threw me back on myself, and yes, on my friends, in "the movement." We had been there early on, so to speak, and so no one was asking *us* anything about ourselves. We had our flaws, our blind spots, our moments and longer of meanness, pettiness, parochialism, moodiness—yet somehow we managed to get on, to accommodate ourselves to one another, to live and let live, or in the clutch, to bring one another, necessarily, up short.

But increasingly we became well-known, caught in a moment of history. Foundations sought us out—and reporters and people carrying television cameras. We became, collectively, budding institutions, with not just a room here or there, but a big "office," with typewriters and many phones and people who didn't just stop by for a Coke and some rest and food, but who came to work at typing and issuing press releases and dealing with officials who worked in other (public or private) institutions. We were becoming (some veteran activists at, say, 24 or 25 kept insisting) all too much a part of the "power structure." I will never forget a comment made by one of those young people, a black man from Demopolis, Alabama: "Hey, listen, these people who want to sift through us and sort us out, and shrink us and test us—who are *they,* and what do they *know* about what we *are!*"

He was exclaiming rather than asking; he was turning the tables on some of us, making a distinction between knowing and being, demanding that we look closely at ourselves, our own assumptions and values and ideals—never mind those of others. Over the years I have learned, sometimes quite reluctantly, to be grateful for such moments: the skepticism of certain moral visionaries directed at my ilk. To be sure, there is always reason for someone like me to help others (religious authorities, for instance, as well as political activists), figure out which volunteers or applicants or would-be associates seem likely not to turn out suitable. So doing, we may help such inquiring people, such applicants, in the long run, rather than be instruments of their rejection.

Yet I appeal for a skepticism that ought be directed at some of us—my kind. I shudder as I think of someone like me sitting and watching and questioning a young Dorothy Day or a Rosa Parks or a Martin Luther King Jr. We are certain, *now,* that they were the finest of human beings. Yet, in the beginning they were called all sorts of names, and not only by their avowed enemies—even as John of the Cross and Teresa were sources of great trouble to many of their co-religionists. Those severely censured one minute in time (and psychology or psychiatry are sometimes today's instruments of condemnation in the hands of various conformist "principalities and powers") can emerge, in another moment, heroes, martyrs, saints—or just good, good people, misjudged in their idealism, their religious or moral passion, by the rest of us, who never think we might be the ones who require a careful look or two, not by a doctor, but by our own consciences.

December 1984

Small Gestures

A student in considerable distress came to see me a couple of years ago. She was a freshman. She had taken my undergraduate course in the fall semester. Now it was April, and she was ready to quit Harvard College. I asked her why. At first she spoke of the general difficulties she'd experienced as a particular young woman—someone who grew up in a factory town, whose father worked on an assembly-line, having never finished high school, and whose mother hadn't either, because she went to work in a department store, full time, at 16. I tried hard to explain to her that things would change, that she would feel more comfortable with a strange and occasionally forbidding place over the course of time.

I also tried to address the matter of class—a young person's understandable anxieties as she tried to comprehend and get along, day after day, in a world of wealth and power. "I know," she told me at one point, "that I'm not the first person who's poor and who's managed to get through this school, but I don't seem to have what it takes." She paused, then emphasized her conviction with a terse repetition: "I just don't have what it takes."

We went on further. I asked her the usual questions someone like me thinks to put before his students in trouble. Had she made any reasonably good friends? Had she found any enjoyable activities? Was there a possible field of (academic) concentration which tempted her? She had, indeed, found a friend or two. She had always liked to sing, and so she had found pleasure in the university choir. Yes, she liked history, especially American history, and she would major in that—if she stayed. But she doubted she would. Why? She pulled back from our conversation when I asked that question. Soon she was sobbing, and I was nervously, guiltily trying to figure out what was wrong—with her, and quite possibly with me as someone trying to be of help to her.

Eventually I heard this: "I've had some terrible times here. The worst of them is being a cleaning lady for some of these rich guys here. They are unbelievably arrogant, and I hate this way of earning money." As part of her "scholarship package," she scrubbed the bathrooms of other students. I could certainly agree with her; and had long advocated that *all* students be required to do such work—lest, yet again, the prerogatives of money assert themselves baldly in this everyday manner. "What it comes to," she pointed out to me, "is that the poor here sweep up after the rich. And they keep talking about a 'community' here, and we're all supposedly part of it."

Still, I wasn't convinced that the *general* situation we'd been discussing quite accounted for the mix of agitation and sadness and bitterness to which I felt her giving expression. Finally, just as she seemed ready to go—she had begun to leave her chair—I heard more sobbing, and saw her settle back, now holding on with both hands tight to the armrests. "Let me tell you what happened," she began. Then I heard this: "I've been involved with some political action here. I joined a group that's trying to help poor people—encourage them to register to vote, try to help them with their problems: dealing with welfare officials and landlords and bureaucrats in the hospital when they have to go there. In some of the rooms I clean I meet these really snotty people, and while I'm straightening out their messes, I think of the poor people I've met here in Cambridge, never mind the ones I've known all my life, like my own family and our neighbors.

"There's one room I clean where I thought I could at least feel a little better—a sort of oasis. The guys in that room are real liberal. They write for the *Crimson* [the college daily newspaper]. They write great editorials and book reviews. They're always telling all of us who read them how rotten *apartheid* is in South Africa, and how rotten our foreign policy is, and how unfair Harvard is in some of its policies—the way it buys up real estate and doesn't respond to the needs of the people who live in those buildings.

"One morning I came into that room, and I got talking with one of those guys. He showed me his latest editorial, and it was wonderful—a real powerful attack on the State Department. He had all these great posters in his room—denouncing South Africa and reminding you how much hunger there is in Africa and Asia. The next thing I knew he was asking me all these personal questions;

and then I began to feel uncomfortable, and then he was propositioning me, and then I tried to stop him and get away—well, I had a tough time. He was a real skunk! He had a foul mouth on him. I got out of that room, and ran back to my dorm, and I was shaking I was so upset. First I wanted to go home right away. Then I just sulked. The worst of it wasn't that a guy was putting the make on me: don't misunderstand. The worst of it was that *he* was the guy. I felt as if I'd been betrayed. I felt disappointed and cheated. I felt as if you can't trust *anyone* around here. I thought to myself: some people around here talk the best line in America, and everyone thinks they're the best people in America, or the smartest, anyway (including the professors, who give them As); and then they go and act this way, like snotty animals, out to take what they can get, and who cares how someone else feels about it."

She gradually began to realize how much she had learned—without question, the hard way. She began to realize that being clever, brilliant, even what gets called "well-educated" is not to be equated, necessarily, with being considerate, kind, tactful, even plain polite or civil. She began to realize that one's proclaimed social or political views—however articulately humanitarian—are not always guarantors of one's everyday behavior. One can write lofty editorials (or "diary" entries!) and falter badly in one's moral life. One can speak big-hearted words, write incisive and thoughtful prose—and be a rather crude, arrogant, smug person in the course of getting through a day. In this regard, I remember a Nicaraguan *commandante* speaking noble and egalitarian thoughts to my sons and me in Managua—and meanwhile, my son noticed, he pressed buttons, secretaries came and went, bringing coffee, and never were they acknowledged, let alone thanked.

Character, my father used to tell me, is what you're like when no one's watching you—or, I guess, when you forget that others are watching. Dickens, as usual, was shrewd about this sort of irony in our lives—a tragedy, really, for us—when he used the expression "telescopic philanthropy" in *Bleak House* to describe what the student quoted above had witnessed: someone whose compassion for far off South Africa's black people was boundless (and eagerly announced to others through the act of writing) but who could also, near at home, behave toward another person as shamelessly as any South African bureaucrat might contrive to act.

No wonder Jesus spent his short time with us doing those everyday acts of charity, offering those small gestures, emphasizing the importance of the concrete deed—the pastoral life. Let those of us who find that words come easy, and who like to play with ideas, and call the attention of others to our words and ideas, beware. Our jeopardy is real and continuing.

January–February 1985

The Hero Without and Within

I'd like to discuss "heroism"—with the help of a few individuals I keep remembering and mentioning in these columns and elsewhere as I try to figure out what this life means and what matters in it. I well remember the first time I heard the word "hero" used in connection with a person I knew; the one making the designation was Martin Luther King Jr. and he had in mind, as he talked, a six-year-old black child, Ruby Bridges, who had been walking past heckling, menacing mobs day after day in order to attend a New Orleans elementary school (William Frantz). The white children had been abruptly withdrawn when Ruby first arrived; so she was alone in a classroom with a teacher herself reluctant to be working "under this awful federal desegregation order," she told me. Yet, even that teacher would one day agree with Dr. King—acknowledge how singularly impressive this child had proved to be in the course of her initial year of school. Dr. King had called Ruby "a hero of the civil rights movement." The teacher would not come to that conclusion, but she certainly specified some of the personal qualities she had seen in Ruby, and did so by remembering incidents, telling stories, rather than summoning the abstractions of social science.

"I don't know where that little girl gets the courage," she commented one day. Then she confessed, in this manner, her continuing struggle to find the answers to that implied question:

I watch her walking with those federal marshals, and you can't help but hear what the people say to her. They're ready to kill her. They call her the worst names imaginable. I never wanted "integration," but I couldn't say those things to any child, no matter her race. She smiles at them—and they're saying they're going to kill her. There must be 40 or 50 grown men and women out on those streets every morning and every afternoon, sometimes more. One of the marshals said to me the other day: "That girl, she's got guts; she's got more courage than I've ever seen anyone have." And he told me he'd been in the war; he was in the army that landed in Normandy in 1944. He said Ruby didn't even seem afraid—and he sure remembered how scared they all were sailing to France. I agree with him; she doesn't seem afraid. There was a time, at the beginning, that I thought she wasn't too bright, you know, and so that was why she could be so brave on the street. But she's a bright child, and she learns well. She knows what's happening, and she knows they *could* kill her. They look as mean as can be. But she keeps coming here, and she told me the other day that she feels sorry for all of them, and she's praying for them. Can you imagine that!

Meanwhile, I was talking with Ruby, trying to comprehend her conduct, marveling at her apparently stoic and certainly brave endurance. She was, she kept telling me, "just trying to go to school." When I expressed my chagrin at what she was experiencing, she observed that she loved being in school, loved learning her "letters" and her "numbers." When I wondered whether she might be afraid (she never *seemed* afraid, much to everyone's amazement, her teacher's especially), she didn't say she was, or she wasn't—but rather shifted the ground of our discussion this way: "I do what my granny says; I keep praying." My mind was not at all satisfied with such a response. She was being evasive. She was "denying" her fear, pushing it out of her mind, I suspected. So I'd been trained to think: such courage, such heroism—a behavior enabled by the "mechanisms of defense" employed by the ego.

My wife, however, had another point of view—kept reminding me that we all use those "mechanisms of defense," but not all of us end up being a Ruby, or a Dr. King, who knew well that various haters wanted to kill him and told his audiences that he knew so, and surely experienced his fearful moments (as I heard him with such lovely candor and modesty acknowledge again and again to those working with him in the early 1960s) and yet who (rather like Ruby) kept praying, kept doing—well, what? Here is how I heard Dr. King answer that question: "You ask about the 'psychological burdens' of living the way we've been living here in the South! When people ask me where I get the courage, or how I can keep standing up to these mobs, I say the answer is very simple: I can't *not* do as I'm doing! There is no alternative, you see."

I fear that it was hard for me to "see"—even as my kind, trained in psychoanalytic psychiatry, has a far easier time probing psychopathology than appreciating the sources of strength and vitality and resiliency in the ordinary lives of people, never mind in the lives of our various heroes. I remember, as a matter of fact, a challenge made by Reinhold Niebuhr to a class of his I attended: what would we do, were we at Union Theological Seminary in 1939, when Dietrich Bonhoeffer, of aristocratic Aryan stock, then studying there, announced his intention of returning to the Third Reich, in order to take up arms against Hitler and his thugs? The consequences of such a move, Niebuhr reminded us, were all too clear at the time—arrest, confinement to a concentration camp, the possibility, probability of death. What would we have made of Bonhoeffer in 1943 or 1944, were we German psychiatrists—at a time when Bonhoeffer was imprisoned and "all" the Nazis wanted was a recantation, a willingness to reverse his stand, join their ranks, as so many doctors and lawyers and professors, and alas, ministers had been doing, including men who taught "ethics" and "moral reasoning" at universities and seminaries? (To get an A in a course in "moral reasoning," Dr. Niebuhr reminded us, is not to prove oneself able to live a decent, a moral life, let alone show oneself prepared for courageous action.)

The implication of such a line of questioning is evident: the usual categories we summon to describe people, to explain their motives and purposes, can be rendered utterly inadequate by particular moments of crisis—by wars, by upheavals of one kind or another, in which life itself (the social and psychological situation of millions of people) has become abnormal, meaning thoroughly at variance with what usually obtains. Under such extraordinary circumstances a new psychology, a new sociology can get going.

Neither Ruby nor Dr. King, nor, I believe, Dietrich Bonhoeffer, regarded themselves as "courageous," as "brave," as "heroic." They regarded themselves as, finally, with their backs to the wall—with no choice but to act in the way they did. These were individuals not only of high conscience (plenty of us talk a good line about our noble ideals and values) but of demanding conscience—a voice within that (at a minimum) said there is no pathway but *this* pathway, and a voice which was heard by the person in question. (Ruby kept telling me she simply couldn't forget what her "granny" told her—that if she prayed, God would listen, and give her the strength she needed.)

At certain times some of us experience a kind of transcendence which may well defy the reductionist, deterministic mentality of contemporary social science. I remember Dr. King quoting the wonderful remark Flannery O'Connor made: "The task of the novelist is to deepen mystery, and mystery is a great embarrassment to the modern mind." His mystery was, of course, Christian to the core in its wellspring. So was Ruby's and, yes, Bonhoeffer's. But others have drawn their mysterious, if not miraculous moral energy from the Hebrew prophets, from Islam's powerful teachings, from the haunting, instructive silence of Buddha. Still others have found in their loved one, their buddies in war, the source of incredible dedication, zeal, and ultimately, self-sacrifice. Mothers and fathers who would hate to die, and yet would immediately give themselves up to death for the sake of their sons and daughters, perhaps can imagine what happens in the field of battle—whether the struggle be military or political. Moreover, at times an ideology, or a certain struggle's proclaimed intention, becomes a loved one of sorts—a nation, a race, a unit in the army, so beloved as to merit all possible jeopardy. "I can't imagine my life without this struggle," I heard from one of the civil rights activists who nearly got killed in Mississippi during the 1964 summer in which several hundred such youths faced down the murderous Klan of that state once and for all.

For such a youth, the reward for his courageous stand was historical—the change in the South's politics, America's. He also liked being admired by those he knew, though there was plenty of embarrassment when the praise became rather effusive and persistent. Ruby was spared such a trial; in the years of her childhood she simply kept going—was not honored or celebrated, within her family or by her neighbors. Only when she was an adult did a grateful New Orleans, much changed by then, say a thank you to her.

The martyrdom of our Bonhoeffers and Kings has, sadly, given them no problem, so far as the matter of integrating a heroism into a later life. Surely the egoism or narcissism we all have is challenged, as it were, by a public commemoration of what is so often an intensely private matter—the consequence, really, of a given person's immersion (by fate, by change, by decision) in a given "existential" situation, with the outcome of that encounter, of course, unpredictable at the start, and often realized only afterwards for its significance by the individual in question. No wonder I heard certain brave souls in that Mississippi Summer project feel *ashamed* that they lived (whereas three of their comrades died), and declare themselves anxious not to be treated as heroes. The very conscience which sometimes drives people to risk their lives does not relent afterwards—rather, makes them feel sad or guilty or worthless, however irrationally, with reminders that others have died while they live.

Still, some do manage to rejoice in what they have done, not out of vanity or self-importance, but in an almost humble recognition that, really, they were the instruments of a cause, a nation's destiny, an ethical struggle, a people's needs. And all the while the rest of us pay close attention, feel the awe, the curiosity, the wonder—and ask about ourselves: what might we do when and if this or that extraordinary, exigent moment falls upon us?

March 1985

The Gift of Thomas Merton

I have been reading Michael Mott's recent biography of Thomas Merton, and remembering the strong and continuing influence that Trappist monk exerted on many of us who read him first in 1948, when the autobiographical *Seven Story Mountain* was published. I was 18 at the time and in college. I had a strong interest in 19th century English novelists, and in American and English history. I was taking courses by Perry Miller, who was a brilliantly original reader of the 18th and 19th century New England Puritan writers and preachers—but whose own religious life (he once told me) was "more a matter of reflection than faith." I can still hear him saying those words; I can still see the twinkle in his eyes—the detached and wry look, and too, the intellectual pride that a particular man knew to flourish in himself.

It was Perry Miller who told us to read *Seven Story Mountain*— pressed it upon us with obvious conviction. I can recall my first effort to comply, and my distinctly mixed response—admiration for a lyrical writer and skepticism with respect to his message. I was, at the time, all caught up in the promise of another kind of message, that of psychoanalysis, and kept wondering whether the author of this book (at 33, some 15 years older than I was at the time) ought not have sought a psychiatrist's help—a way of "working out" all the obvious troubles described in the book.

As I give the foregoing account I feel embarrassed and ashamed, and yet I am not so sure Merton himself didn't confidently expect, as he penned his account of his still young life, such a response from people of my (American, bourgeois) generation—for whom psychoanalytic psychiatry was a newly arrived secular preoccupation, to say the least. He himself had done some reading of Freud and other psychological theorists, and later in his monastic life would have a sad and fearful and all too instructive encounter with one of them, the far from modest, the singularly tactless, the thoroughly smug Gregory Zilboorg. I note, now, my anger at Zilboorg's arrogance and considerable stupidity in his approach to Merton—instructively reported in the Mott biography. (Merton had been having grave spells of self-doubt, if not despair, and a meeting with that well-known psychoanalyst was arranged.) Yet, I wonder whether (as a young psychiatrist) I would have regarded Merton all that differently; and even today, I struggle as I read of Merton's life, or that of other Christian writers—struggle to keep at bay one or another all too confident psychiatric formulation meant to explain why it is a given person acts as he or she does.

In Merton's case there was plenty early childhood sorrow. His mother was an American artist who married a New Zealand artist, had two sons, Tom and John Paul, and soon enough got sick with cancer. Merton was only four when she died. He had a major and persisting memory, all his life, of a rather aloof, but intensely scrutinizing woman who apparently kept a journal of sorts, in which she recorded the baby Tom's various activities and small, day-to-day achievements: his first word, his first moment standing up, his first steps—the memorable victories so many of us parents have learned to witness with awe and remember with powerful nostalgia.

Merton himself was perplexed at times, in his later life, by his insistent interest in keeping watch on himself, so to speak, through the written word: those journals he kept and kept (and used as the basis of his many books) as well as the enormous correspondence he maintained. It is no great or surprising feat, I suppose, that one of my ilk, trained to make psychological connections between the past and the present, would comprehend the later Merton's passion for an essentially autobiographical writing as a response to the young Tom's experience with a writing mother whose subject was Tom.

Yet, once I have come up with that observation, I have nothing much to offer—yet another late-20th century doctor or social scientist who has figured out a "factor," a "variable" in someone's life. We've all had our parents, and they've exerted an influence on us—and I suppose it is worthwhile that we know and understand the significance of such an influence. What interests us about Merton, however, is not his rather unusual and melancholy early life (and its continuing shadow upon him as a grown man) but the powerful intellectual, moral, and spiritual force he exerted on a generation of readers, Catholic and non-Catholic.

He was, really, a constantly changing person—and years in the monastery did nothing to stop that process, for all the enclosing, demanding steadiness of the monastic routine. He came to the Trappists already much lived—his mind exposed to Marx, Freud, a wide range of novelists, poets, moral philosophers, and his body no stranger to wine, women, and song. (He was a great jazz aficionado.) His still widely read autobiography touched a major post-World War II nerve—the disenchantment of many members of the Western middle classes with various secular promises. Merton was yet another prominent convert, yet another reminder that "the hound of heaven" may well catch anyone, no matter his or her sophistication, privilege, and apparent disinterest in matters religious.

In a sense, the young convert Merton was a source of great pride to the older, conservative U.S. Catholic Church that preceded John XXIII—as I well remember realizing when I listened to the mother of my closest friend (he is now a Jesuit). She was constantly praying for my conversion to "the Church," and she had, in fact, sent me *Seven Story Mountain* well before Perry Miller got around to pressing it on his students.

Yet, the later Merton was a bit harder for her to take. Her conservative politics, conventional religious piety, and love of tradition in the Church prompted nervousness, even fear, as she began to realize how *bold* Merton could be, how *outspoken*, how responsive to the many social and political currents of an increasingly restless and fast-changing America: the late 1950s and 1960s. As Merton embraced his various causes—*our* various causes—she wanted from him silence, conformity, the old, familiar prayers and pleas tethered to the old sentiments. Instead he became increasingly troubled by the predicament of the South's black people, then turned critical of America's intervention in Viet Nam, and too, our nuclear militarism. And he a Trappist! A Trappist, she had always thought, ought to have other matters on the mind!

Still, she (and so many others) could not ignore or forget Merton. He was a powerful and persuasive writer. Moreover, many who had read his autobiography had given themselves to him, it might be said, in an exceptionally full and unforgettable way, and so there was a bond not easily broken. No wonder, then, a priest's mother who was particularly religious (in the old-fashioned, immigrant Irish sense of the word) kept reading Merton, kept struggling with his "new ideas" (she called them), and in the long run, kept learning from him about the contemporary life of the Roman Catholic Church.

In Merton the Church had a wonderfully able and convincing teacher—one who embodied a transition that took place in Rome (Vatican I and II) and America (the Church we now know). In Merton God gave us yet another gift of His grace: that of an anchor in rough (political, social, spiritual) seas. It is ironic that such a rootless and wandering youth would end up, in his later years, being for so many of us such an anchor of faith!

April 1985

Silone's Religious Humanism

Each year I look forward to the lectures I give on the life and work of Ignazio Silone—and especially, on the significance of his singularly affecting novel, *Bread and Wine*. As I take up that book, yet again, I often think of Dorothy Day holding it in her hands. She loved Silone's writing, and stood in awe of his brave, complex, utterly honorable life. In the 1950s, when I was a medical student and did volunteer work at a Catholic Worker "hospitality house," I was always on the lookout for writing that would take me away from technical, scientific writings that were, anyway, hard for me to comprehend. Again and again, in talking with Dorothy Day, I heard Silone mentioned, his complex and decent and visionary life paid respect, his wonderfully spirited and compassionate writing celebrated. "I would lend you my copy," Dorothy Day told me, referring to *Bread and Wine*, but she just couldn't part with it, she explained with embarrassment: "I keep thumbing through pages. It's one of those books that keeps coming back to you!" I would learn, eventually, which books prompted her to such possessiveness: Tolstoy's and Dostoyevsky's novels, one or two of Dickens's.

Several times she gave a few of us her modest but thoughtful and knowing expositions of Silone's life—in itself the stuff of a 20th-century novel. He was born in Italy (1900), the son of a peasant. His mother was a weaver. Even as a child he was sensitive to injustice—the power the rich exerted on the poor. In 1915 he witnessed the devastating consequences of an earthquake—50,000 people killed in eight seconds. He could never banish the memories of the local bishop quickly leaving the area of devastation, the memories of food being denied some, hoarded by others. He had, of course, been reared in the Catholic Church, but now began to

122

see its not rare intimacy with corrupt, if not evil, "principalities and powers." That image—of a fancy prelate beating a safe retreat, while thousands of his flock lay dead, with thousands of others homeless, starving, and in full despair—haunted him throughout his life: a scandal, and a continuing aspect of Christ's suffering. In 1944 he would write: "In the sacred history of man on earth, it is still, alas, Good Friday."

But before Silone would embrace such images, he would try to forsake religion altogether, and become a passionate, self-sacrificing Marxist revolutionary. As such he had to abandon his given name, Secondo Tranquilli, in favor of Ignazio Silone—the latter of the two pseudonyms chosen as a gesture of respect to Q. Pompaedius Silo, a rebel of ancient Rome who fought on behalf of the disenfranchised. All during his own life Ignazio Silone struggled on behalf of our century's disenfranchised—the vulnerable and hurt people (the *cafoni*) he knew so well.

He was first a socialist, later a Communist—a comrade of Gramsci's and Togliatti's. He was editor of *Lavoratore (Workman)* published in Trieste, a fiery newspaper devoted to the struggles of Italy's workers. In the 1920s, his 20s, he went to Spain and France on various Communist political errands, and ended up in the jails of both those countries. By the middle 1920s he was a leading Italian Communist, and so, a delegate at an important international Communist meeting: the Congress of 1927—a turning point in the history of Russian Communism, one gathers from various accounts rendered, including his, first published in *Communita* in 1949. The monster Stalin was then beginning to consolidate his grip on a nation and a worldwide political movement. Silone saw not only the struggle between Trotsky and Stalin, but the betrayals, the lies, the widespread cruelty—all justified by an ideology that claimed historical and moral immunity for itself: even murder, never mind double dealing and slander, justified in the name of the "revolution," or the "proletariat." Silone's account of his eye-opening disenchantment, one of the first in the history of modern international Communism, was eventually published in English as a chapter in Richard Crossman's collection of essays *The God That Failed*.

Needless to say, Mussolini's Italy offered no home to Silone, and after his break with Stalinism, he found his way to Switzerland— and to a career as a writer, novelist, and essayist. He would pen a number of novels, starting with *Fontamora* (1933), and later on *The*

Seed Beneath the Snow (1941) and *A Handful of Blackberries* (1953).
But his greatest novel is *Bread and Wine,* published in 1937, when
mankind seemed headed for the darkest spell ever—with the likes of
Hitler and Mussolini and Franco and Stalin seemingly what was in
store for the world in the foreseeable future. This novel's central
figure and hero, Pietro Spino is named for Pietro da Morrone, the
Benedictine monk and hermit who, nearly 80, was summoned to
Rome in 1294 to become Pope Celestino V. In a few months he
abdicated, the only pope to do so—his devout and holy qualities,
his innocence and utter devotion to prayerful contemplation, not
quite what the Vatican seemed to need. He was canonized in
1313—a statement by the Church, surely: saints are not to be
confused with the rest of us, including Church authorities.

Silone was constantly fascinated by the life of Jesus, by utter
goodness as it shone upon a world saturated by evil—the confident
light He shed upon a tenacious darkness. The Pietro of *Bread and
Wine* is a revolutionary on the run, a victim of a failed and flawed
secular (Communist) politics—now hounded by an equally cruel
and corrupt (fascist) counter-politics. The fugitive takes on the
disguise of a priest—a brilliant stroke of Silone's, and perhaps the
single most important announcement he would ever make: the
yearning in his heart and soul for a revolutionary kind of Christianity, as in the early communitarian Church, when its members
lived radically egalitarian lives, ever skeptical of power, privilege,
wealth, and conventional authority. This Pietro, only pretending to
be a Catholic priest, is in spiritual truth just that—an intensely
good and generous man who in his own way follows the Jesus of
the Galilean sermons.

The novel is, really, a series of scenes—Pietro's encounters with
the poor, the well-to-do, the pure of heart, the embittered, the
disappointed: the full range of humanity. Even as Jesus walked
among us, addressing our hopes and fears, our darker side and the
brighter possibilities within us, Silone has his story's central figure
abandon political and economic abstractions (their attendant risk,
so often, is ideological self-righteousness and arrogance) in favor of
those small, concrete, pastoral moments which are so utterly redemptive. The world is wolfish, devouring, full of evil, Silone
knew—yet, good will and love are also constantly in evidence:
God's gift to us. *Bread and Wine,* with its evocation of both sides of

our human experience ("the children of light, the children of darkness") offers and embodies Silone's powerful religious humanism: the secular radical who was, all along, one of Christ's generous-hearted faithful.

May 1985

Further Thoughts on Abortion

The longer and harder I put my mind to the issue of abortion—
what to think of it, what to think of my values as I contemplate its
significance—the more I feel myself all too immersed in the assumptions of this contemporary world. In an earlier column (Oct. 1983)
devoted to this issue that troubles so many of us, I tried to describe
my personal responses, as they have changed over the years: the
young physician whose reformist liberalism prompts him to think
about the desirability of abortion for the pregnant and poor women
he meets who are already trying to do the best they know how, and
who (he is sure) don't want any more children, and similarly for
other women, pregnant by incest or rape, and still others in fragile
health themselves and afraid of the medical consequences of a
pregnancy—as against the person who now remembers with sadness his inability during those years to appreciate just how eager
some of the women he knew were to bear the children they were
carrying, no matter the opinion of people like me.

What I really was discussing, I'd better acknowledge, is the
gradual transformation of a point of view. Back then moral judgments passed the muster of my secular mind. I worried about the
physical health or emotional state of particular women patients. I
worried about the young victims of rape and incest I met in a
women's "reformatory" where I worked for awhile (The Lancaster
Industrial School in Massachusetts). I worried, more generally,
about "the poor," the "population problem," the "Third World,"
about the vulnerability of all sorts of uneducated and hurt and
ailing people—the essentially abstract concerns that affect (to vary-
ing degrees of intensity) people like me, sheltered by privilege here
in the United States.

I think I'd still today mainly be thinking along those lines (and to some extent, at least in part, I always will) had it not been for the abrupt shift in my life's direction and work in the early 1960s, when I became involved, full-time, with black and white children going through the South's school desegregation crisis, and with the sit-in movement in that region. In essence I stopped being a physician, a child psychiatrist, whose time was bought by well-to-do members of the liberal intelligentsia (a not unfair description, I think, of the families who seek the advice of my ilk who practice in Cambridge, Mass.) and instead spent my time with ordinary people, mostly poor or from the so-called working class, whose lives had suddenly become touched by fear and anxiety—by the dramatic onset of a historical moment. Now I was regularly sitting in homes and sometimes, alas, in make-shift cabins, with the "poor," and, yes, with families in which there were large numbers of children. Now I was seeing, first-hand, people whose lives, whose social and economic and political fate, I knew to deplore from afar. Now, slowly, I was learning about "them"—and maybe about myself, my own ideas and preconceptions.

I still remember, for instance, a particular couple my wife and I had come to know well. They lived in a small Georgia town. They were black, and hard-pressed in so many ways. They had six children. He worked in a store, a handyman. She scrubbed the floors of the local bank at night, and tried hard to be a good mother during the day. She was, I realized, not in the best of health—she had suffered through a fairly serious bout of rheumatic fever as a child, and the result was an impaired heart valve, and episodes of congestive heart failure. I will never forget the day when this woman told me that she was pregnant yet again. She wasn't utterly ecstatic; she knew the burdens she was already carrying. But she did have a smile on her face; and her mind was not dwelling on herself, but rather, on others: "My two big girls [they were then 11 and 13] are going to love this new baby. They'll want a girl. They're tired of the four boys we have! We'll get another plate and put it on the table. That's what my momma used to say: 'We're going to have a visitor, a new person God is sending here, and He's chosen this family and so let's put a new plate on the table and say welcome.' And like her, I try to teach my children that it's God who has sent them here, and it's up to us to show Him we're grateful. If He's chosen us to have another of His children stay with us, then we'll manage, and we'll be better for it, I truly believe, even if it'll be hard. Yes sir, it'll be hard."

I doubt I'll ever forget that afternoon conversation or my perplexed response as I drove away. Phrases such as "planned parenthood" and "birth control" raced through my mind. I kept thinking of the "ignorance," the "cultural deprivation," the lack of "resources"—the "factors" or "variables" that relentlessly pressed upon a particular woman and her husband and her many children. She, on the other hand, had in mind God's will—and, yes, a community's hopes and pleasures: the satisfaction her children would feel, and others too. "I know our minister will be glad," she told me, "and so will my sister, because she's [pregnant] with child now, too, and [when she finds out she'll say] they'll grow up together."

The more I reflect upon that woman's words and deeds (and, Lord, I have met others like her here and abroad) the more I have to look closely and candidly at my own ways of seeing various aspects of this life. Whereas she regarded herself, when pregnant, as the recipient of a gift from God, and certainly (she often told me) as the custodian of a life "growing every day inside," as she put it, for me the matter was at once abstract (the sociology of impoverished, semi-rural black Southern life!) and when personal, thoroughly a matter of this individual woman's situation—her health, her impoverished circumstances, her "needs" (a better deal all around) and her "rights" or "desires." Even when she didn't give expression to those "desires" I took it upon myself to declare them present—in the back of her head, of course! With more "education," maybe after a spell in an office with someone like me, she'd realize what she "really" felt, realize her frustrations and resentments. Then, of course, she'd think as I do—and be declared in possession of "insight," and on the way to a "cure"! Or was I the one who needed a revelation or two—a glimpse at the philosophy of egoistic individualism that was working overtime as I drove away from that humble black woman's home?

An abortion for her, then, was unthinkable, and would be so now for her daughters, whom I occasionally visit. (They are themselves mothers.) An abortion for her would be the deliberate taking of life—and as she put it so often, "life is God's to give, and ours to have and treasure until He calls us back to Him." She was part of His community, and her forthcoming child, really, amounted to a visit by Him! Her mind, her life merged constantly with the lives of others—not only God's life, which she heard celebrated in church, but the lives of all the people she knew. I kept trying to remove her in my mind from her "religious preoccupations," from her grim "socio-economic setting," not to mention the racial oppression she had surely experienced all her life. I wanted her thought processes to work differently, I suppose it could be said—so that, maybe, her daughters would one day have more freedom, live better lives. Her aspirations, however, were centered on another kind of future— that of the Kingdom of God, she once told me. The poor benighted woman! Or is it I who needs pity and lots of prayers? Meanwhile, I've kept in touch with that girl (it turned out to be) she was "carrying" back then, and oh, Lord, I'm glad she's alive and with us—a wonderful young Atlanta nurse in training.

Everytime I hear the subject of "abortion" discussed I think of her and her mother—and me and my big-deal secular kind, all too smugly influential, and I fear quite capable of being blind on various scores, including the matter of abortion: blind because we attribute to all others our own self-centeredness, even as many human beings regard themselves, above all, as members of a particular community of human beings, one headed by God Almighty.

June 1985

Walker Percy's Christian Existentialism

Among American novelists of the second half of the 20th century, Walker Percy has chosen an especially difficult terrain to work, to explore. He is no casual storyteller, no Dixie romancer who wants to spin smart, lively yarns. He is a physician and a conscientious, erudite student of philosophy, who has known life's down side (when he was 12 his lawyer father committed suicide, and when he was in his middle 20s he became seriously ill with tuberculosis). He is also a man much interested in religious matters. At 30 he converted to Roman Catholicism, and he is known to show up in the Catholic Church in Covington, Louisiana, north of New Orleans, where he lives, and sit there meditating and praying—on a weekend morning when no one else is there, the priest included. His novels are meant to be not only entertaining and funny (and they are) but serious examinations of our contemporary, American bourgeois life—a risky venture, because an intellectual and ethical ambitiousness of purpose can all too easily weigh down badly a particular effort, turn it into a thinly disguised textbook, full of assertiveness rather than the delicate suggestiveness a good novel offers.

The great success of Percy's first novel, *The Moviegoer*, was in part a consequence of a certain stubborn determination on his part—a refusal to become authoritative and demanding, the familiar posture of the secular expert, so often trained in some social science, who wants to take over the stage, mesmerize the audience with a lot of postulates and pronouncements, and be declared a (passing) guru. Rather, *The Moviegoer* is a restrained, even wary evocation of our contemporary, American, secular, upper-middle class situation—the nature of this life many of us live, with all its mysteries, confusions, uncertainties. Percy knows that we are the creature who uses language, whose distinctive glory (and tragedy) is consciousness, who asks in all sorts of ways those utterly rock-bottom existential questions—as in the Gauguin triptych: Where do we come from? What are we? Where are we going? But Percy the novelist doesn't aim to give us a pedantic or precise answer to such a line of inquiry—a series of psychological or sociological formulations, say, to which we would all eagerly and compliantly give our assent. In every one of his five novels the narrative voice is the same, a wryly amused spectator who misses little with respect to the hypocrisies, banalities, and plain stupidities that pass for contemporary "relevance"—the self-help books, the self-preoccupation of an affluent intelligentsia, or yuppiedom, "the great suck of the self," as he puts it at one point.

He is, really, a spiritual diagnostician who also happens to have a wonderfully alive and sharp sense of humor, a major probing instrument for his spiritual analysis of our modern age. Where others are all taken up with particular and obsessive polarities—left against right in politics, traditional as against radical in human affairs, conventional as against thoroughly "free and easy" with respect to so-called social or family matters—he is likely to see, sadly, the shared assumptions so many of us have, no matter our ideological tilt. Smugness, arrogance, self righteousness, a pervasive egoism—these are not the property of any one political party, or the attributes of those who espouse any particular cultural or social or economic viewpoint. They are qualities of mind, and alas, heart, which ancient preachers—as in Ecclesiastes, as in Isaiah, as in Jesus and His disciples—knew to be constant threats and temptations for every single one of us. In a memorable scene in *The Moviegoer,* Binx Bolling, the befuddled and increasingly knowing, if not wise, seeker sits in the library and peruses our various secular magazines and spots all too exactly the pretentiousness and occasional conniving that gets called serious or important writing. In the novel *Love in the Ruins,* Dr. More, the failed doctor whose soul just may be saved one day, sits and contemplates the craziness of some not so distant future, the antics and postures of our various and mutually antagonistic social and religious "movements." In *The Last Gentleman,* Will Barrett moves across America (North and South, East and West) and finds no evidence at all that any of our various regional or sectional enthusiasms, preferences, predelictions have in any way given any of us exemption from all the sins of omission or commission human beings are wont to find tempting.

In every Percy novel there is a complex, religiously sensitive yet also modern and scientific sensibility at work—a narrator who knows his medicine, his psychoanalytic psychiatry, and who knows what physics and chemistry have meant for us in this second half of the 20th century, this last waning spell of the second millenium: all sorts of "breakthroughs," yes, but still the old Adam is us, with meanness and spite and phoniness and greed in no way diminished by the burgeoning knowledge of the physical or social sciences. Percy's characterization in *The Second Coming* of one person as someone who "got all A's and flunked ordinary living" tells a lot about his own moral outlook. The novelist and person who makes such a distinction is asserting a major irony, to say the least—that "smart" is not necessarily "good," that lots of big shot intellectuals are thoroughly vain and ethically wrongheaded. And all through Percy's philosophical essays, collected in *The Message in the Bottle* and *Lost in the Cosmos,* that theme gets asserted loud and strong— the failure of so many highfalutin, secular, messianic fantasies, while still we keep searching for answers to those old existentialist questions that are at the heart of things: what does life mean, and how in the world ought I live that life?

For Percy it was Jesus who gave us the answer—the one religion, His, which offers us "God become man." Jesus gave us His life in several senses of the expression—gave us those messages, those Galilean parables and paradoxes, those urgent sayings and strong remonstrances, those loving gestures and demonstrations of concern: a Life for all eternity to contemplate and call upon as an example. Percy's existentialism is unmistakably Christian—that of the "wayfarer" he mentions from time to time who has taken notice of a particular visitation we here on the planet earth received nineteen hundred and eighty five years ago, and accordingly, drawn the necessary and personal conclusions. For those of us who get perplexed, if not outright disgusted by the many faddish causes, the creedal pronouncements pressed upon us by a parade of secular authorities, Dr. Percy's presence among us, his stories and essays, are a significant gift, indeed: an aspect of God's grace meant to give us nurture, help us smile, hold our heads high—keep our sights on Him, and not those who behave as if they aim to be His successors.

July–August 1985

The Spiritual Life of Children—
Part I

The constraints of culture are often invisible; they coerce us, but we don't think of them in connection with our ideas, our values, our inclinations, our likes or dislikes. Twenty-five years ago I was talking with black and white children in New Orleans; they were going through the ordeal of school desegregation—amid considerable street violence, shouting mobs, and an attempted white boycott of the two elementary schools to which a mere four black children had been assigned. I was interested in how a black girl of six (from a very poor family) who is heckled and threatened every day manages to get on—her "adjustment," as we know to put it these days. (I have, I know, referred to this in earlier columns.)

As white children slowly came back to school (for awhile one black child, Ruby, was at school all by herself) I talked with them too—wondered about their sense of things as they took part in a significant moment of historical change. Trained in pediatrics and child psychiatry and psychoanalysis, I did my job by talking with the children or playing games with them; by asking them to draw or paint pictures and discussing with them, thereafter, what they had in mind as they did their art works; by talking, too, with their parents and teachers.

I had in mind, of course, certain notions of what happens to children under stress—the "defenses" they mobilize, the "symptoms" they sometimes develop. These were not flimsy or foolish notions, and I do not mean in any way to deny their legitimacy, so to speak: the years of arduous, painstaking clinical work that can enable someone like me to make all sorts of helpfully instructive and clarifying observations and interpretations—the heritage of a particular culture, in this case, the medical and psychiatric side of that culture. Still, as I watched those children, asked them my questions, recorded their answers, made my surmises, and came up with my conjectures about the future, I was myself being watched, and conclusions about me were being made—by the children I was getting to know, by their mothers and fathers, their uncles and aunts, their grandparents.

One day in New Orleans—I'd been working there for over a year—Ruby's mother, Mrs. Bridges, had given me a Coke, and felt comfortable enough, at last, to sit down with me at the kitchen table and initiate her own line of conversation, rather than (as had been the custom) wait a bit, tensely, even fearfully (I began to realize), for my questions, my stated concerns. She asked me about my education, and I explained it to her—the various years spent in various places. She did not, however, let the matter drop there. She asked me about the questions I'd been putting to her, to her husband, to Ruby—and again, I patiently tried to explain to her that it was important to know how Ruby's appetite was holding up, and whether she was sleeping soundly, and what she said or did under various sets of circumstances. She nodded, and then told me, reassuringly, that she appreciated quite well my interest in her daughter, and realized that I was trying to see how her mind and body were responding to an extremely stressful time—but she did want to say something to me that had been on her mind off and on. I waited for her to speak, but to no avail. I decided to encourage her, and when I did, I heard this: "You're the doctor, I know. I shouldn't be asking you questions. You know what to ask children. But my husband and I were talking the other night, and we decided that you ask our daughter about everything except God."

She stopped and looked down at the floor. I was at a loss for words. To be honest, I didn't really understand, at the time, what she was talking about—and so I started doing what people like me so often do! I worried about her "mind," her "psychiatric status," her "educational level." I thought to myself: this fine and hardworking and honorable woman is, alas, quite poor, and has had virtually no schooling (she couldn't write her name or read), and she is now quite worried about the harassment her child, indeed her entire family, is experiencing, and so is grasping at straws, showing a certain naivete or gullibility or superstitiousness.

This talk about her daughter and God, this observation that I wasn't asking their daughter about God—I'd never heard such a comment before, and I could only guess about its significance: an all too religious mother (I knew how loyally the family attended church) preoccupied with the notion that some prayer, that faith in God, would get her family through a tough ordeal.

Not that I was scornful of such an attitude. By then I'd come to know Dr. Martin Luther King, Andrew Young, and a number of other black ministers and civil rights activists. I'd gone to Dr. King's church, to many other black churches in the South, and I'd learned to appreciate their everyday, compelling significance in the lives of thousands upon thousands of black people, then and for decades, indeed, centuries before that time.

Once, in a bemused moment, as he sat and tried to explain a number of aspects of black life to me, Dr. King said tersely, "Don't overlook the fact that there are now only a few thousand of my people enrolled in the civil rights organizations here in Atlanta and elsewhere—but there are many millions of us enrolled in the Baptist Church, and other churches." He went on to tell me, gently but firmly, that he "sometimes" had to keep declaring that fact to many of his friends, "especially the ones from the North, who want to help us but don't really know much about our religious life, and don't have much of a religious life themselves." He was not being critical, or even mildly sardonic—simply the good and earnest teacher, thoroughly appreciative of the people he'd described, but aware of any number of differences between their lives and those of his parishioners, and countless others who flocked on Sunday (and indeed, other days of the week) to pray—and pray and pray, with remarkable dedication, persistence, passionate intensity.

In fact, as I sat there in New Orleans, silent and uncomprehending, and yes, worriedly suspicious (what did Mrs. Bridges mean, and why was she saying *that?*), I thought of this earlier conversation with Dr. King—as an explanation of a mother's remark I otherwise found worrisome, if not bizarre. Even so, I was mute with concern as well as confusion. Why did *I,* as a doctor, a child psychiatrist, have to ask Ruby, or any other child, about God? I didn't dare put that question to Ruby's mother; instead, I fumbled for words, and when they didn't come easily, I resorted to the old familiar ploy, the verbal tic, the arrogant mannerism people like me have at their disposal: "Would you explain what you mean?"

She had no trouble doing so, quite concisely: "God is helping Ruby, and we thought you'd want to know that." I must admit: I decided to let the matter drop. I was a doctor, I was studying children caught up in social stress, in a racial crisis, and best to stick with my notion of how to go about that study. I changed the subject—asked yet again about Ruby's eating and sleeping habits, her comments about her school work. Never again did Mrs. Bridges broach the subject of God in that way to me. Indeed, I remember thinking to myself: I'm studying the *psychological* life of children—not their spiritual life—and that was that. In my next column I'll continue examining my thinking over the years, and try to make clear why I have come back to that moment in New Orleans, again and again.

November 1985

The Spiritual Life of Children—
Part II

I mentioned in the last column a distinct and memorable unease that came over me when the mother of a black child of six going through the daily terror of a mob-opposed desegregation in New Orleans (during the school year 1960–1961) took me aside and asked me why I hadn't yet "asked" her daughter "about God." My wife, as she read that column, was rather blunt with me, and I guess I'd better put down, here and now, what she said: "You're being a little blurry around the edges here! I remember you telling me about that moment—and you thought that Mrs. Bridges was a little loony, or simple-minded and naive. You laughed at the idea of asking a child about God. You said: 'I can picture the look on my old supervisors' faces [the child psychoanalysts who were my teachers during my residency years at the Children's Hospital in Boston] when I tell them about my conversations with boys and girls about God.' You said—I remember—that Mrs. Bridges was quite frightened by the mob, and she was telling . . . you how frightened she suspected Ruby was, too, by suggesting you talk with her about God."

There was more—the gist of it being a wife's clear memory of a husband's psychological reductionism: if the Bridges family was interested in religion rather intensely, if Ruby was preoccupied in any way with God, then there was a *reason* for it, and that reason was, ultimately, *psychological*: a frightened and anxious child calling for God's protection. Or perhaps the reason was *sociological and cultural*: the child was the product of a given "socio-cultural background," for whom "religion" and "prayer" and "god" are words or "practices" handed down in keeping with certain "traditions" or "rituals."

138

I use those quotation marks to indicate an abstract, intellectual mind at work—the social science variety: my way of thinking as I got to know certain children over two decades ago. To be sure, when I had spent a bit more time with such youngsters and their parents I became a bit more "tolerant" and "understanding"—so I flattered myself in thinking. I had realized eventually (hadn't I?) how "useful" it was for the Bridges family to pray, to attend church—how "functional" it was, "psycho-socially." I had decided that certain "superstitions" (or to use the word Freud did to describe religion, "illusions") have at least a passing "value" in the history of civilization—a crutch of sorts for families with very little else on which to lean.

Not everyone (one whispers to oneself in all candor) has the knowledge and self-confidence and insight (of course!) to resist the blandishments and temptations of the "infantile" or the "primitive" aspects of the social world, as they impinge upon us. Nor can everyone take for granted, one hastens to add, the social and economic circumstances that enable a certain calm, reflective, knowing attitude toward this life—so, out of one's privilege (and self-congratulatory pride!) one feels sympathy for "them," for all those poor people, all those uneducated people, all those people who have never had psychotherapy, let alone psychoanalysis, all those men, women, and children who are in dire straits, and driven to the various forms of behavior which desperation and vulnerability press upon human beings.

A few years "down the line" (of this perplexing wayward life!) I had moved to yet another posture; now I was astonished at what had happened, say, to Malcolm X: his first conversion from a life of crime to the Black Muslims, and his second conversion, with its attendant evidence aplenty of a Christian sensibility at work—the charity and kindness, the forgiving nature one sensed and witnessed in him. By then I was less sure of myself—less willing to throw around ideas and concepts and theories in order to "explain" Malcolm X, not to mention Dr. King, and too, others whose obscurity (in contrast to Dr. King's celebrity) made them no less brave, decent, determined, and, not least, morally upright in the way they lived their lives. (How upright are some of us who sling around fancy language, and have an interpretation for everything and a categorization meant to put anyone in his or her proper place?)

It was at this time that I started writing about Malcolm X, about some of the humble, hard-pressed folk, black and white, I had met—about their resilience and fortitude, yes, and always about their psychological lives; but also about their moral qualities: the thickly textured ethical life they lived, at times awesome in its everyday significance.

I remember writing to Anna Freud, for example, about Malcolm X, asking her what she thought accounted for the sudden shift in his life—from "confidence man" and jailed "psychopath" or "sociopath" to fiercely obedient and articulate Muslim, and then, to gentle and loving person who urged decency and charity upon all of us. She was interested, indeed—and quite willing to tell me this: "We know, more or less, how to account for what goes wrong in people; and we know how to account for certain links between early experience and later behavior—but we don't know about the miracles that take place, and I don't only mean the big ones. In so many people you and I can recognize one, maybe more, of those miracles as having occurred—in people who have gone through terrible times, and yet are fine, fine people, and haven't turned 'bad.' Meanwhile you and I will be thinking of people we know who have everything in the world, it seems, and they are weak psychologically, or if not that, then far from inspiring in their personal lives, their morality. There is a lot we don't know.

"As for the religious forces you mention, I wouldn't know how to account for their influence on Malcolm X, or anyone else. This is a subject for study, and we may not even know how to do such study, not yet. But I do agree with you: I wouldn't want to discuss the religious life of anyone—the two conversions of Malcolm X you have cited—as merely evidence of psychopathology. I can see how you would be worried that some of us in psychoanalysis might want to do so—*have* done so; but you must give us the same room for growth and change, the same respect for our individuality, that you have been so determined to give to those Southern children and those ghetto children of the North you've written about! Maybe in time we'll understand more about these matters—what makes some people so much more impressive (not only stronger psychologically, but more impressive as human beings in their behavior with other human beings) than we understand now. Maybe we'll even come to understand more about the way people use religion in their lives. But I don't expect to see that time soon. That is a project for the future, like so many others!"

Those hard-to-forget words have resounded in my head since 1972, when I first received them. I suppose I needed Miss Freud's sanction to begin to think a bit differently about the religious and spiritual life of children—to think about it as a part of their life, well worth comprehending *on its own merits, with its own dignity* and *significance,* rather than as a "reflection" or "expression" of this or that, a consequence of one or another (causative) antecedent, of various personal events, or of the given social and cultural and economic situation in which the particular people in question are immersed. So far so good—though, there is more, I fear, to tell, and so in the next column I will pursue this matter yet again.

December 1985

The Spiritual Life of Children—
Part III

In two previous columns I discussed some of the practical and theoretical difficulties I encountered as I did my "field-work" (as those many home visits with children get called these days) in various places over the past two decades. I was trained at a time when being "value-free" was an ideal much to be sought. "Value-free psychoanalysis," "objective research," these were buzz words in the late 1950s as I was doing my hospital residencies in psychiatry and child psychiatry. I have already indicated in several earlier columns (before I began this series of three on "The Spiritual Life of Children") how much I would eventually learn from some of the poor, embattled children I met, and from their parents, too; and how puzzled I was by the more than occasional evidence of courage and virtue and wisdom I found in them—my surprise, of course, being a measure of my preconceptions and ignorance, meaning the constraints of the fancy and lengthy education I'd received. I was looking (I'd been trained to look) for "the mark of oppression" (the title of a psychoanalytic book published in the 1950s dealing with "the Negro personality") and instead I found people of stoic dignity, often enough making do rather shrewdly, patiently, and thoughtfully against great odds. Not that some hadn't become wayward, badly so—but then, not a few people of great means and considerable education also fall behind psychologically, even become villains of one sort or another.

Eventually I decided to study the moral involvements of children, and too, their political involvements or interests—a way, I thought, of moving from a strictly psychiatric point of view. I use

142

the word "involvements" because I was *not* primarily interested in what children *thought* about this or that moral principle or political idea. Piaget and others have been quite exhaustively helpful in that regard. I was drawing a distinction (I'd been taught to do so by the children I'd come to know) between what boys and girls (not to mention the rest of us) *think* and what they actually *do*. One can respond with the utmost brilliance to the moral scenario presented by a researcher ("What would you do if . . .") and still, in everyday life, be a fairly mean or selfish or self-serving person. I keep quoting Walker Percy's remark—"one of those people who got all A's and flunked ordinary living." By the same token, I had to come to terms with, say, Ruby, who at six wasn't capable of any fancy, clever "moral reasoning" or "ethical analysis," but who prayed hard and long and daily for the mob who tormented her: "Please, dear God, forgive those people, because they don't know what they're doing."

No matter the psychological reasons for such prayer (fear, anxiety, and so on), the girl managed the deed. Of course, some of us can deliver brilliant lectures on ethical matters, write our books and articles, and not find such a child's humble forgiveness in ourselves, and indeed, be thoroughly arrogant and insensitive, for all our analytic powers. Such ironies are no surprise to novelists—indeed, they are the stuff of so much fiction. I think I began to realize, in the mid-1970s, that I'd better follow the "methodology" of those novelists—set down what I'd see, and not try to banish life's inconsistencies and paradoxes with various expressions of theoretical legerdemain.

I went back, therefore, to children I'd once known (now much older), and I sought out other children, in an effort to document the moral actions (or lack thereof) of young people here and abroad. Now I was more open to the psychological complexity of those children's lives—less ready to be psychologically reductive in thinking about what they did and why they did it. But I have to say that I still had my troubles with some of those children, still couldn't bring myself to try to understand, on its own merits, their religious life, their spiritual life. Not my province to explore, I thought. When, for example, a black child of six told me that she was sure that "the Lord was watching" her tormenters, assembled in a street daily, and so she herself would "try hard not to think bad of them," I concentrated first in my thinking on the *psychological* side of things (the child's struggle with anger). Later, as I tried to reconsider what I'd seen and heard over the years, I concentrated on the *moral* side of things (the child's critical restraint with respect to her would-be assailants, and indeed her ultimate compassion for them, as embodied in her prayers to God on their behalf).

Yet, I am only now beginning to realize that I still have a way to go, if I am to understand that child, and other children the world over, who pray hard and long to God, go to church, and attend Sunday school, or who may not be of a conventional religious background, but who have (as one boy of 12, the son of a college chemistry teacher, told me he has) continual speculations about God: whether He exists, and if so, in what form, and what He might wish of us with respect to the way we live our lives. Those prayers or ruminations or expressed questions, musings, reflections are aspects of what I think ought be called the spiritual life of children—*not* mere expressions or symbolic manifestations of psychological conflict or moral reasoning. Similarly, the child who reads the Bible, and listens to the Bible being read in church, and can't get out of his mind the passage that tells of "how hard it will be for some people to get into that little, little hole you can barely see in a needle." Similarly, too, with an "adolescent" who is struggling with her personal life, yes, and with her moral life, yes—but who also finds herself paying close attention to some of the more compelling moments in the New Testament, and particularly the scene ("I can't stop imagining it") when Jesus "really spoke up against hypocrites and phonies, you know, in Matthew, the 23rd chapter."

A powerful chapter indeed, that one, I thought to myself as I heard the comment—at the time, though, a mere distracting moment in an interview that had, so I thought, more important purposes: to pursue a youth's psychology, her moral development. Both objectives were worth pursuing, but so is the matter of this youth's manner of seeing the world, the imagery she summons, the references and symbols she finds significant, the stories and analogies she summons constantly, the segment of world history, of human experience, she uses in her personal thinking—a spiritual world that is hers, and needless to say, not hers alone. We "experts" in America need to listen and look more, to let those whom we "study" become our teachers. We who are interested in the young need a "phenomenological" research into childhood experience—

an approach that doesn't try to impose all sorts of sociological or psychological constraints upon what is *there,* wanting to be observed, and only later "evaluated." William James dared regard religious life seriously—indeed, with the respect one ought feel for those intent on living up to their possibilities as human beings. We need to follow his example with children, too—not study their spiritual life reductively, or with condescension, or any ulterior motive, but in Reinhold Niebuhr's memorable phrase, in order to discover what we can about "the nature and destiny of man."

January–February 1986

Don't Worry, Dad

The three boys are gone, I say to myself. The boys are no longer boys, I remind myself. I go to their rooms sometimes, look at the tangible evidence of the years they have spent on this planet—please God, with their mother and me: the little cars and trucks they delighted in having when they were five or six, now tucked away on shelves inside their closets, with one or two still left here and there in a particular room for them to see in a quick glance as they go on to other matters; the books, some going back to the days when they listened to us doing the reading, some the first objects of their newly achieved literacy, some the works of art that link so-called youth with so-called grown-ups, such as *Animal Farm* or Kipling's stories or those of Hemingway or Mark Twain, and finally, books such as *Invisible Man* or *Pride and Prejudice* or those convoluted Henry James novels. All this tells their English teacher mom and novel-loving dad that we're four voters now, and one soon to be, and that two are away in college, and one soon to be, and that everyone drives, and we all wonder, out loud, what's happening to America and the world, not who can come over and play Lego, or when that Red Cross swimming instructor will be able to hand out those junior life-saving cards.

I catch myself sad one morning. I think as I go from room to room of the missed chances, the missteps, the misstatements—things done I should not have done, things not done I should have done. Why didn't we help the first boy to make more friends earlier? Why did we keep him so close to us? Yet, he has lots of good friends now, and is quite comfortable traveling all over, I remind myself. *Still*. Why did I get so impatient at times with our second son? Remember that day when a friend came, and the three-year-old child was running all over the place, and fell down and

146

cried, and I was in the middle of a conversation I had judged to be "important," and I shouted, and the child cried harder? Yet, he's a strong, even plucky young man, no crier, and he is thoughtful, and while he doesn't interrupt people, he also doesn't seem resentful or gloomy in his willingness to hear them out; and he knows when to speak up for himself. *Still*. Why, finally, did I miss some of those wonderful school celebrations the third son wanted me to join, or avoid talking with some of his teachers, because (I told myself) I was shy, or I felt my wife could talk better with people in the neighborhood, in the school. Were those self-told jokes about my hermit-like nature a transparent excuse for my pride, my egoism: stick with the writing, the teaching, where the control is yours, and the subject matter, too, directly or indirectly? Yet, this high schooler and I have a great time talking about Latin or biology or a theme that is due by the end of a given Monday. *Still*.

I say to myself, having visited all three rooms one day: "They've turned out fine." Then I arraign myself as all too full of myself, as summoning three other creatures of God for my own chronically self-serving purposes. They *have* turned out fine, I say now—but (in the tradition of a 20th-century secular world obsessed by a meliorism heavily saturated with psychology, with dreary phrases such as "child development," "parenting skills," "learning environments") they might well have turned out even better. Wasn't one boy too reticent too long in school? Didn't he take years to relax among his classmates, known these days as "peers"? Wasn't another boy a little too neat and orderly for a while, and much more relaxed with his mother than with me? Hadn't we worried a lot for a year or so about the third child's sloppiness and his preoccupation, we deemed it, with those rock albums? A half an hour or an hour, occasionally, is alright, I'd thought, then said (and to him, not only to myself and his mother), but on and on the playing of those records went. Besides, the teachers say he comes to school sloppy— or rather (I corrected them silently and with sinful pride) manages to turn sloppy within moments of arrival there.

If only I'd been with the boys when younger more of the time! If only I'd not been so taken up with my work, my damn research—all that "field-work," all those "home visits" to other people's homes, all those children interviewed, again and again, other parents' children. No wonder I think back wistfully at all the opportunities forsaken, the spells when I was traveling, or worse, plain self-preoccupied. Would I be sad that these three boys are now just about grown up, if I'd been with them more than was the case? *Really* been with them—concentrating all my mental and physical energy on their lives, the way their mother has done, with great enjoyment. (She: "They needed you to leave, to do your work. They'll always love and respect you for it." He: "Don't say that—it's a rationalization, a justification. A pity it's all over now." She: "It's never 'over'—even when we die. We remember a lot of each other, all of us do, and there were all those good times we had, *you* had." He: "There could have been more. I feel sad, bad about that.")

The other day I got upset about some stupid matter, and once again, stupidly, compounded an initial stupidity by adding to it my own stupid shouting. I slammed a cabinet door shut, a dish precariously placed fell and broke, I shouted even more—whereupon one of my sons said: "Don't worry, Dad." I found myself getting angry with him, as I do occasionally with my wife, when she, also, mobilizes a phrase meant to supply some badly needed perspective, both moral and psychological. Then I remembered an event that took place over a decade ago. The same boy had cut himself badly, and I had to rush him to the hospital. He'd cut an artery at the wrist, and I was speeding. He was sitting beside me in the car, quietly—with a certain detached interest, actually, in what was happening. I was not only upset at the traffic—the emergency allowed me to consider everyone driving to be perversely slow, or dim-witted, or obstinate, or childish, or senile—but at the boy. How many times had I told him to stay away from that drawer, with all those dangerous tools! He'd already hurt himself with the hammer. I thought we'd settled the matter then—that he ask permission to use anything at all in the left-hand side of the chest. Certainly he was old enough and sensible enough to understand me at the age of seven. Wasn't that the age of reason!

There I was, cursing the failures of the drivers of Concord, Massachusetts, while my own mind was in the above described manner proving itself to be plain crazy—and outrageously, wrongheadedly moralistic. Nor was this the only time such a way of reacting had taken place; nor was this to be the last time I would turn mean and sour in my thoughts, in my face's expression, and ultimately, in my language, when confronted with a difficulty experienced by one of my children. My own father, sadly, used to give me hell when I did something wrong that caused injury to me.

There I'd be, hurt, bleeding, in pain, and he'd shout at me: why did you do that? What's the matter with you—can't you listen and remember?

In the long stretch of psychoanalysis people like me go through (a big help in learning how to understand ourselves and others), such childhood troubles come up and get examined repeatedly, and so eventually I figured out that my father's outbursts had to do with his nervousness and fearfulness. He was scared by the trouble I'd presented to him, worried I might be in jeopardy (I broke a few bones when I was a kid, sustained my fair share of bruises, infections) or yes, worried I might be in great discomfort (I got poison ivy regularly and in bad attacks), and he put such worries in that immediate form of expression: "Why, *for Christ's sake,* did you go near that poison ivy? How many times have I showed you what poison ivy is? What's the *matter* with you?"

My mother would then get angry—at him. Her Christian ire was aroused by the swearing—but really, she was aghast that the victim was being blamed: "Will you, *for Christ's sake,* leave Christ out of it—or if you have to mention Him, remember what He stood for!" That was enough to silence him. Yet, I remember feeling the pain of his momentary, reproachful lapse longer than any caused by the actual illness or accident I'd happened to suffer—and no matter how quickly my mother had managed to intervene. In fact, I remember times when my mother's anticipated intervention worked so well that my father said nothing—but a telltale look in his eyes was there, and that was all I needed to feel dopey and wayward, well worth a stretch of gloom.

I vowed over and over never to repeat all that with my own children, and yet I was, on occasion, helpless—then devastated by my helplessness, and utterly disgusted with myself. Thank God, actually, for those perfectly normal drivers who roused me to rage that day: I got to the hospital faster on their account, because they stimulated me to dodging and zooming and using my horn—*and* they kept my mind, mostly, away from my son's predicament, meaning in this instance, away from grave temptation. I believe the psychoanalytic phrase is "repetition-compulsion." Soon enough we were at the emergency ward, my son's wound was sutured, and he seemed fine. But as he got up from the table and saw something cross my face, he was moved to say something: "Don't worry, Dad." With these words a smile, finally, broke across my face, and we were able to have a pleasant drive home. I think I crawled back in the car—glad to enjoy the sights and sounds of a particular day. I remember being startled when somebody passed me and gave me a dirty look.

On another occasion, with another son, I recall raising my voice, saying what his teachers had said, that he was not using his mind enough in school, his "God-given intelligence"—talk about parental narcissistic grandiosity flimsily masked (and rationalized) as exhortative, necessary piety. The boy was in the seventh grade, and had been goofing off. Nothing doing, I'd thought—but kept my silence. When the teachers spoke, though, I followed. But my previous, frustrated silence had exacted a cost: I shouted. I was angry for other reasons, too, and so the usual controls had given way. Complaints from me pounded forth: the messy room, the messy way of dressing, the willingness to pay complete, abjectly submissive attention to a "them," all those fellow twelve-year-old slobs—and *this* boy, who had always seemed so "independent," so eager to follow his own idiosyncratic interests: fish tanks, mechanical gadgets of all kinds, splendid forays, even then, into stories and novels and nature essays (Lewis Thomas) and the literature of travel (Steinbeck, Theroux).

When I'd had done with my tirade, I slumped into a chair, and then all of a sudden, without warning to myself, started crying. I guess I'd never heard myself speak like that to a child, any child, never mind my own. I got up quickly and left the house and got into my car and drove and drove, this time, oblivious of all other drivers. On the road I passed our family's favorite ice cream stand, Bates Farm—a splendid, homemade product dispensed against a background of grazing cows, a silo, fields of hay, a colonial New England farmhouse. I am an ice cream freak, and this was the moment for a big hunk of mocha chip—but I couldn't drive into the Farm's parking place. Somehow it seemed obscene of me even to want to gratify such an impulse—to soothe my ailing, hurting soul while that of another deserved the comfort far more. When I came back, my wife saw the look on my face, and knew exactly what to say: "Don't start in with that 'I'm sorry' routine! What you said was right, and he needed to hear it." Needless to say, as if she were a confused driver in my way, I got angry at her. I was ready to argue and argue, but realized I'd best shut up, disappear: the exile of the study, morally sanctioned by the requirement of work to do. But I could only stare out the window and feel rotten. Soon my wife was calling us all to supper, and she has never allowed grudgy or grumpy static to linger. Her cheer (I call it "forced" when I'm reluctant to let go of pride's despair) quickly swept us along, as did her delicious supper of spaghetti and baked chicken and strawberry rhubarb pie. Later the boy and I were taking some garbage to the barn, and I prepared to apologize. Only the next day did I realize how readily I'd been comprehended and anticipated. I'd scarcely opened my mouth with the words meant to affirm, in a long-winded explanatory statement, a given mistake, when I heard "Don't worry, Dad." I recall feeling like a small child who'd been forgiven, and who now could feel better. I recall my eyes filling up. He and I went to Bates Farm and got our cones.

I tell you, I say to myself sometimes, with more of those tears choking at me: to be a father is to love one's children, love them continually, love them enough to give them countless kisses and boosts, examples and assistance; but also love them enough to stumble with them, before them, on their account, love them enough to say the wrong things, do the wrong things—not because, God save us, some damn fool American "expert" told us *that*, too, but simply by reason of one's humanity put on the line, one's frailty and helplessness exposed. To be a father, moreover, is to heal those children over and over again, hold them and hug them and carry them on one's shoulders and on one's bike and beside one in the car, healing them daily as they sustain daily the world's inevitable, constant assaults, and in so doing, be healed by them: Don't worry, Dad—meaning, thank you, and I'm glad you're here to fall down and say "the wrong thing," because Mom is right, I did need to get that message, or because it's nice to see the next guy (especially when he's a passing demigod, as all parents are for a while) come down to earth—hence what we boys have been telling you ever so casually yet with conviction, time and again: Don't worry, Dad.

March 1986

Remembering Reinhold Niebuhr

When I was in medical school at Columbia's College of Physicians and Surgeons, I had a difficult time with the laboratory science that dominated the first two years of medical school. Several times I went to see the dean and told him I was unable to continue. Each time he persuaded me to stay—at least until I got on the wards, when an entirely different kind of education obtains. On my last grim visit to that dean, at the start of my second year, I was convinced that no words of his would deter me: I didn't belong where I was and, having done miserably in my pre-medical college courses, I never ought have been admitted to a medical school in the first place.

But the dean was a formidable person, and his strong Presbyterian outlook was hard for me to oppose. He lectured me as my parents would—about my responsibilities to others, about the opportunities I would soon enough have. When he saw that this time he wasn't getting far with that angle of approach, he changed tack by asking me what I would do when and if I did leave medical school. I had no answer, really, to that question—but in order to fill an embarrassing silence I blurted out an answer that surprised me more than it did the dean: I might try to study at Union Theological Seminary. True, I had studied the Puritans rather thoroughly as an undergraduate (my advisor was Perry Miller and they were his major subject of inquiry). But what in the world would I do at Union, I caught myself thinking as I heard what I'd said? The dean, however, was quite interested. He told me I should pursue the matter, and offered to help. Soon he had me in touch with David Roberts, who taught at Union, and he in turn took me to hear Reinhold Niebuhr teach and preach.

I stayed in medical school, but I was also thoroughly taken with

Niebuhr's brilliant, wide-ranging mind. He was the most extraordinary of preachers—a powerfully compelling delivery, all extemporaneous. As a teacher he called upon history and politics with great ease—and had a wonderful eye for the paradoxical, the ironic, the ambiguous. In medical school everyone sought answers, the more precise and clear-cut, the better. Especially in the psychiatry lectures, those answers were unequivocally spelled out: the early 1950s heyday of psychoanalytic determinism and orthodoxy. But Niebuhr was not one to embrace any secular fad, however persuasive its hold on the intelligentsia. His Midwestern populism, his Christian egalitarianism, and his early socialist days had in no way made him susceptible to the ideological side of Marxist thought—not to mention its Leninist and Stalinist entrance into history. Early on he saw not only the scandal of totalitarian murderousness rationalized as a necessary historical "stage," but the scandalous blindness of those liberals and radicals who ought to have known better than to have apologized for it. What Silone tells us in *Bread and Wine*, Niebuhr had been saying all during the 1930s, and continued to say after World War II: namely, that Communism the world over represents a terrible betrayal. Only gradually (and sometimes reluctantly) did many of his liberal and radical friends come to see this.

For Niebuhr, the concept of irony was a major scholarly and polemical instrument. His keenly biblical mind enabled him to move from the ironies and mysteries—the surprising turns of fate worked into the Christian parables—to the equally unsettling surprises of contemporary history. He was, too, a penetrating moralist—in the tradition of Jeremiah, Isaiah, and Amos—ready always to scorn any number of principalities and powers, including those of the various Christian churches, for their hypocrisies, their stated banalities, their deals with various liars and crooks known as social or political leaders.

I vividly remember him talking about Dietrich Bonhoeffer's decision in 1939 to return to Germany to take up resistance to Hitler. Bonhoeffer might easily have remained at Union, where he was when war broke out—become an outspoken anti-Nazi emigre, lionized by many Americans. He might, too, have maintained a discreet silence with respect to Hitler and his thugs—and lived well in Germany: he came from a distinguished Aryan family. Instead, he chose the extremely dangerous course of opposition—and at a time when the Nazis were riding high in Germany, and about to conquer almost all Europe. Niebuhr reminded us how readily Bonhoeffer might have called upon various secular justifications for a decision to stay out of the way of the Nazis. Indeed, when Bonhoeffer did make clear that he was returning to Germany, a number of quite sophisticated friends (and learned Christians) felt he ought go see a psychiatrist. Did he have a "problem"—some "need" to suffer, to be punished? How convincingly, alas, psychiatric concepts lend themselves to our use and abuse—become the rationalizations and excuses we happen to find congenial! The history of Christianity—indeed, the history of mankind's moral struggles with all sorts of evil—is full of those whose brave and daring breaks with the conventional, the so-called "normal," would all too easily have earned the worried attention of any number of today's psychiatrists, were they somehow sent back in time with their various diagnostic categories in hand.

During his lectures Niebuhr constantly asked us to step back from the influential assertions of this century—to shun the secular certainties so many of us find appealing. He gave us, instead, a wry and detached look at our history—while all the time refusing to let such a point of view turn into sour cynicism, or an excuse for social and political inaction. Above all he stressed our sinful side—the pride, the egoism that constantly attends us—while at the same time reminding us that such self-centeredness ought not be granted sway over us, as in that philosophical surrender that goes under the name of skepticism or a wary resignation in the face of this life's negatives. A moralist, he kept fighting hard to make the world more decent and honorable, to help those who badly needed food, clothing, shelter—even as he never doubted that all reforms carry with them new possibilities for evil as well as for good. His was a dialectical mind, ever ready to examine anew any given proposition, theory, dogma—and ready, too, for the ironical topsy-turvy nature of things, yet again, to assert itself. We badly need his way of looking at politics and religion—his capacity to spot the fake and pretentious and glib, and the wonderful mixture of the conservative and radical in his thinking. He struggled against various American powers, but also turned his sharp eyes on himself and his fellow social or political activists, whose cant and arrogance signify, yet again, the inroad of egoism, of the sin of pride, of self-importance, upon those who fight them as traits or qualities of mind and heart in others.

May 1986

William Carlos Williams:
A Doctor's Faith, a Poet's Faith

When I was a college student I wrote a long paper on the poetry of William Carlos Williams. He was then (1950) by no means the giant figure in American letters he would only become posthumously—when numerous awards were tossed at his memory. (He died in 1963 at the age of 80—and so he had waited in vain for a long time to receive a nod or two from his writing colleagues.) I was a senior at Harvard when I wrote my essay, and my advisor was Perry Miller, who had given years of his life to a study of the New England Puritan tradition. I had hoped to pursue a similar line of inquiry myself—study early American Protestantism through recourse to history and literature rather than theology. But Miller must have sensed some restless anarchic energy in me, because he kept telling me I'd "enjoy" Williams's poetry—no matter that important figures in Harvard's English Department at the time had no great affection or respect for him! "You'll like him; he gives hell to the Ivy League, and to lots of other fake ornaments of secular America," I was told.

I did like Williams's writing. Eventually I got to know him, and got to witness the medical part of his life. He was an old-fashioned "general practitioner," who labored long and hard (and often enough, for little if any recompense) among the largely immigrant poor of northern New Jersey. When I applied to medical school (no matter my poor grades in the sciences) it was because I'd been much inspired by his example. He was forever being stimulated by his patients—healed by them, I began to realize, with the help of his wonderfully patient and shrewdly understanding wife, Flossie, whom I knew well and kept visiting until her death in 1976. "Bill was always complaining about how hard it was for him—to be a full-time doctor, and to write as much as he did—but he could never have done it any other way," she once told me. She explained that observation with this terse follow-up remark: "He needed those visits to those tenement houses; the people there expanded his imagination, and I noticed over the years how much they healed him."

He had, more abstractly, acknowledged as much several times in the course of our talks. I well remember one visit I made to him. I was a third-year medical student, and was feeling overwhelmed by the sheer volume of facts I had to absorb—not to mention the growing realization of the responsibility a doctor's life demands. He listened to my worries and complaints, brushed them aside a bit impatiently: "Look, the rewards are great. All the time there is the satisfaction of doing something half worthwhile—and being helped to feel better about yourself by the appreciative affection of those you've treated. *They* treat *you!*" He was, himself, quite sick when he spoke those words—hence the poignancy of the next statement he made: "I miss my patients. I need them now. They'd make me feel a hell of a lot better—I know—if I could see them!"

No one who has written about Williams has said much about his religious views, his spiritual life—and understandably, I suppose. He was no church-goer; and he could be devastatingly sardonic as he contemplated the phony side of 20th-century Christianity, not to mention its long and sad institutional history: persecutions, wars, greed and plunder, murders of so many people—all in the name of this or that creedal orthodoxy. He had his own way of saying what the Catholic philosopher Romano Guardini asserted with these words: "The Church is the Cross on which Christ was crucified." Williams's words went like this: "They keep nailing Him—in His name!"

His god was a certain kind of aesthetic beauty—the well-crafted poem as an inspiration to writer and reader both. He knew how dreary this life can be for all of us, how bored and self-centered and self-indulgent the rich can be, and how desperately confused and vulnerable and self-lacerating the poor often are. He also knew how few people read his poems, or anyone else's. Mass consumption of all kinds hasn't done all that much for us, he observed—had, actually, made us addicts: at the mercy of appetites ever so fickle and transient. He would hold out for a small moment of truth, and pray in his own way (pounding the typewriter keys in the evening, after using the stethoscope by day) that the light generated by certain words arranged in certain ways would continue to count for something in this universe that is in many respects inscrutable and beyond comprehension.

His other god, as I have tried to indicate, was service—though he was never self-righteous or pompous as he went about his earnest and humble medical rounds. He hoped against hope—and expected, always, the worst: "There is a curve-ball awaiting every doctor every day! Death always wins in the long run—and so does sin, I'm afraid."

I was always surprised when I heard him use the word "sin." What did he mean by the word—he who was, for all practical purposes, a tough-minded agnostic, a person constantly noticing the self-deceptions and self-aggrandizements that get masked as church-going piety? When he used the word "sin" I wondered whether he was approaching a certain rock-bottom evil we all have—and will keep having, no matter our various accomplishments of mind and matter. Yes—but he had something else to consider, he once told me: "On a bad day, I think the idea of Satan quite believable. You're lucky you were a kid when that fella Hitler began marching across Europe—and so many big shots sang his tune, including lots of ministers and priests. I heard their silence, or their cheers. It was a lesson you hope not to forget."

On the other hand, he could be as sunny and buoyantly expectant as a child whose hunger had always been followed by the satisfaction of a delicious and ample meal, lovingly offered. His poems were "gifts," he once told me—offered him by "I don't know whom," and in turn offered to others similarly described: "I don't know them." But he quickly emended that declaration of ignorance: "I do, of course! There's a chain of circumstance that connects us—a chain of being. Who—if anyone—got the idea of us in the first place (and made the idea a thing: people) I wouldn't know, not at all."

Tone is all-important for a writer, and the tone of that last comment was decidedly humble, even wistful,—as if he'd have liked to have "known," but just didn't. He was not at all being truculently assertive about a posture of (skeptical) ignorance; nor did he want to turn against those who did "know"—who had within themselves a sure religious faith. He was ever attentive to our language and to human suffering. He had learned as a writer and doctor the essentials of our nature: we use words to explore our predicament and to fathom our inevitably melancholy, final prospects—at least on this earth. His dedicated work—the healing, the writing—bespoke a spirituality of considerable depth and subtlety, no matter its fiercely independent nature. His capacity for awe, his sense of life's small but dramatic and telling moments, were also expressions of an actively reflective moral life. It was a life, some of us noted, that sometimes turned surprisingly religious in a quite conventional sense, as in the marvelous poem "The Catholic Bells," one he much liked, and a good one to summon as a conclusion to this brief effort on my part to comprehend, yet again, a pilgrim malgré lui. The poem begins:

> Tho' I'm no Catholic
> I listen hard when the bells
> in the yellow brick tower
> of their new church
>
> ring down the leaves. . . .

And it concludes this way:

> . . . Let them ring
> for the eyes and ring for
> the hands and ring for
> the children of my friend. . . .
>
> . . .O bells
> ring for the ringing!
>
> the beginning and the end
> of the ringing! Ring ring
> ring ring ring ring ring!
> Catholic bells—!

June 1986

On "Liberation Theology"

I do not mean (here and now, at least) to get into a discussion of the complexities of so-called liberation theology, nor to mention the ongoing struggle with respect to it within the Catholic Church. Rather, I wish to describe certain experiences which have come to mind as I have followed that struggle, read pro and con on that "theology"—memories of what I happened to hear and see at one or another time during the recent past.

Most memorable for my oldest son and me was a visit we made to the Vatican several years ago. We happened to become involved with an assertive taxi driver who spoke fairly good English. He showed us around Rome, and eventually took us to St. Peter's Basilica. He was naturally garrulous, and made more so by my son's habit of asking question after question. (He was a college freshman then.) Soon we were hearing a speech about the "rich Vatican" and the "corrupt Vatican" and the "politicians of the Vatican"—after which this question was hurled at us (while the cab swerved wildly, making its inroads on the chaotic Roman traffic): "I ask you—*I ask you*—what do you think Jesus would think of this [a wave of the hand in the direction of Vatican City, which loomed before us] if He were alive today?"

I didn't answer the question. My first thought was of the awful papacies that preceded the present one by centuries—the well-known moral scandals of the Renaissance. But the cab driver was insistent. He launched into a tirade about the existence of the Vatican Museum—all the precious objects there, worth hundreds of millions of dollars—"while every day people starve." He pointed in the direction of the Pope's summer home—and again reminded us how millions of others live, their shanties and shacks in the ghettoes, the *barrios*, the *favellas* of this world. "It is not fair; it is not right; it is not Christian," he exclaimed, and then an exhausted slump and silence, as he prepared to stop, and collect our fare.

My son wouldn't let the matter drop with payment of the arranged sum, plus a tip. He kept referring to the cab driver's remarks as we toured the Vatican, and continued to do so when we got back to America. He reminded me what I knew but now found it harder to forget, in view of what the cab driver had said, and what he, my son, was more than implying—that Jesus lived and died a poor, humble man, mocked and scorned by important people, and that during His lifetime there was no "church," only a band of quite ordinary and vulnerable people who spent their time with the sick, the hungry, the lowly, the unpopular, the outcasts.

Oh, the mind pushes that aside fast enough, remembers the justifications (if not rationalizations) for the Church's various policies and practices, as they began developing shortly after the death of Jesus of Nazareth. Still, my son wasn't interested in those justifications, even as that cab driver had brushed aside the few "explanations" I had tried to offer. Oh, these naive idealists, or impossible purists, or political enemies masked as mordant social and cultural critics (was the cab driver a Communist?)! Man is sinful, one keeps reminding oneself, and it is naive (maybe even perverse) to expect from any institution on this earth, even a Church meant to affirm Him, exemption from that sinfulness.

A year later, all three of my sons and my wife and I were in Brazil, where I'd been visiting a particular *favela* over a span of eight years. We stayed in a Copacabana hotel, made our daily visits to those sad, sprawling tenements that cover certain hills of Rio de Janeiro. My wife, my sons, noticed certain churches in the wealthy sections of the city—and then wondered about the religious faith of certain *favelados* we knew.

We all were especially jolted, one day, when my oldest son, still thinking of our Vatican experience, asked a particular mother (through the pediatrician-interpreter who was with us) what *she* thought of the singular absence of the Church in that *favela*, and its presence in a rich neighborhood below us, to which he knowingly pointed. Before the woman had a chance to reply, my son extended his question: What did she think that *He* thought of such a state of affairs? (As he asked, the young American pointed to the statue of Jesus Christ, His arms outstretched, which stands on a high hill overlooking the city.) The woman was 25 and already old-looking and sickly and the mother of four children. She had no education, no money, no husband; she was kept alive, to be blunt, through the help of a man who himself was barely able to get enough money to buy cheap food. (He begged, washed cars in Copacabana, ran errands.) She was a thoughtful and sensitive person, and in her own way, quite religious—though not the most regular of churchgoers. Her reply to the young American went like this: "I am sure that Jesus prays for them [the rich who live in Copacabana]. Maybe they need the church there more than we do! I pray to Him right here. I look at Him and talk to Him. [She pointed to the statue.] Once we had no food for two days, and I thought we'd all die. I was ready to go meet Him. Then a friend of mine brought us eggs and bread and cereal. All we had was Coca-Cola. I wonder if He would drink it if He came here. It kept us alive! He will tell us what He thinks when we meet Him. It won't be too long! Down there [in the Copacabana and Ipanema sections, to which she pointed] it will be longer before they see Him! They stay here longer!"

A stunning faith—of a kind that people such as us, hearing it avowed, hardly know how to comprehend. She was not interested in the inequities and injustices we found appalling—even though she was living out, day after day, their consequences. She prayed long and hard at times to God, and looked forward to meeting Him. Yet, she was a mother who desperately needed to feed her children, couldn't always do so—and on occasions other than the one described above, could become puzzled, and, yes, quite bitter. At such times she asked the kind of questions my son has asked in recent years, questions such as these: "Why do the rich ignore us, and still they go to church? My sister tells me the priests live well down there [Copacabana and Ipanema] and I wonder if Jesus sees how they live, and how we live. . . . Does He get angry? I hope so! He cannot be bought by all their money—Jesus; I hope they know!" Once, in a more sweeping condemnation, she insisted that the Church "belongs" to her kind of people, not to them, the rich, the quite comfortable—appearances not withstanding.

I have never known what to think or say when I hear such talk, but I can't believe that whatever discussions all of us are now having about "liberation theology" ought not in some way be connected in our thinking to lives such as hers, and, yes, such as that of the Rome taxi driver as well.

September 1986

In Paul Tillich's Seminar

In 1957 I had finished medical school and was trying to decide whether I would be a pediatrician or a child psychiatrist. In order to be the latter, I had to take training in adult psychiatry, and did so at the Massachusetts General Hospital and at McLean Hospital. I did not have an easy time of it. I kept hearing men and women described by various psychiatric categorizations in a rather rote and often haughty manner. Not that those descriptive efforts were necessarily wrong-headed or unhelpful. When I heard a particular person, a young wife and mother, being called "phobic," I was being told something important about her. But there were other aspects to her life that deserved recognition. On psychiatric grounds, never mind human ones, it was important to know her other sides: the thoughtful and plucky and resourceful individual she *also* happened to be. If she was going to make progress in her struggle with her fears and worries, she would need to summon those strengths—and we, her doctors, would have to acknowledge their presence, as well as help in mobilizing them.

The foregoing is obvious to the point of banality, yet was not then so evident to many of us—all caught up, as we were, in the heyday of psychoanalytic reductionism. We were entranced with our ability to use psychiatric labels, to explain everything as the result of certain somethings—those linear extrapolations from event A in point of time A to event B in point of time B which seem to give psychological diagnosticians and practitioners the mighty aura of science. The more ambiguities or ironies we permitted ourselves to notice—I realize in retrospect—the less clear-cut and decisive our sense of ourselves would have been: mere readers, say, of Dickens or George Eliot or Tolstoy, rather than *doctors!*

At that time I was still not sure I wanted to practice psychiatry—

and as I heard any number of psychiatrists talk (and, alas, gossip endlessly about one another's "psychodynamics"), I had increasing hesitations about seeking "treatment" for myself. Instead, I tried to enroll in a seminar the theologian Paul Tillich was then giving at Harvard University, only to find that many others had a similar intention.

Tillich patiently and conscientiously interviewed each of us, and ultimately I was allowed to audit the seminar, I think because he saw a certain sad desperation at work in me when we first talked. To this day I remember a remark of his on that occasion. I had told him what I was doing, and he had smiled and told me of his interest in psychoanalysis. Then suddenly his face relinquished its lively upbeat appearance. He lowered his head and took off his glasses, to clean them—a bit of a tic, I would eventually observe, as if he repeatedly had to find a better perspective for himself. Finally, these words: "Psychiatry, today, is a faith for the faithless, certain ones of them." That remark, especially the last qualifying phrase, was vintage Tillich—the careful and learned scholar who at times realized all too well that he himself had been elevated in the minds of some to the deity: yet another of America's authorities, relentlessly hounded for whatever pontifical assertions he happened to have available at any given moment.

In his seminar he worked us toward a critical distance from the very culture that had lifted him to notoriety—as the theologian sufficiently interested in secular obsessions to be rewarded with considerable attention and flattery. He made clear his respect for Freud's discoveries and Jung's, while at the same time emphasizing not only the considerable gullibility or zealotry of some of their ardent followers, but the acquiescence of many of the rest of us—who scan the intellectual world hungrily for whatever scraps of authoritative explanation of this world's nature we can manage to find for ourselves. One memorable day Tillich went further, hinted at the destructive side of this idolatry: "People are built up in order to be destroyed."

Such a terse remark can itself be evidence of a secular hero's descent to banality—but Tillich knew to expand his thoughts on the subject. He remarked upon the driven or desperate character of the search for "experts," who tell us, all the time, what to think, what to do, when to do it. Even back then our bestseller lists were full of advice books; now they are, surely, the dominant element in

American publishing—a constant flow of instruction on how to bring up children, eat, stay young or healthy, engage in sex, make millions, keep our wits about us, make friends galore, weather various "stages" of this life, and even die with the psychological imprimatur of "healthy" stamped upon us by some minister, rabbi, or priest who seems far more interested in psychology or "pastoral counseling" than in reading the Bible and taking seriously its various messages.

Tillich could be forceful in that seminar—and quite confessional at times. He acknowledged, openly, once or twice, the influence of a skeptical haute-bourgeois world upon his thinking—the seductive power, really, of a society interested in exploring everything and everyone, and believing nothing or no one "for any length of time." That phrase meant a lot to him as he made his critical exegesis of Manhattan (and Cambridge, Massachusetts, and the San Francisco Bay Area, and other centers of knowledge or academic and intellectual power). He understood well the transient nature of critical acclaim for those like himself and, alas, the false nature of the embrace in the first place: ah, let's try an emigré German theologian for a change—one whose interests in "art" and "psychology" remind us of our own, and one whose religious convictions are "intellectual" and "philosophical," hence not likely to make anyone in the 20th-century American upper intelligentsia too nervous.

Tillich saw all that happening—with respect to himself, with respect to many of us. (Every temporary celebrity, whether of the mind or the movies or sports or politics, requires a willing cohort of worshipers.) In that seminar he laughed wryly at his own expense— and I began to realize, smiled at us, who had fought like hell, elbows sharp and flexed, words craftily mobilized, to "get in," and then, to curry his favor. He was praying hard for himself, for us— and by the end of the seminar I think he had helped us all a bit, boosted our skepticism somewhat with respect to American cultural fads, reminded us persuasively that there is only one God, and that only once did He come here to be among us.

October 1986

Physician, Heal Thyself

Doctors are more likely to kill themselves, or become alcoholics or drug addicts, than those who belong to any other profession—a sad and instructive piece of information. I first heard such observations—and the statistics that go with them—being recited when I was a medical student. Even then I'd begun to notice some further ironies, variations on the same theme: pediatricians who spent a lot of time with their young patients, to the point that their own children missed them terribly; somewhat overweight internists who told their hypertensive and obese patients how important it was to lose weight; and not at all to be overlooked, psychiatrists who impressed many of us as being quite odd, if not loony.

For a long time I tried to forget such puzzling aspects of medical reality—or, I'd remind myself that we are all limited, if not flawed, in various ways, doctors included, and so my very surprise at what I was seeing bespoke a naive utopianism at work: the notion that the choice of a particular profession would in some fashion provide a degree of psychological and moral perfection otherwise unobtainable.

When I was a boy I had been taught fifth grade by a teacher, Bernicia Avery, who ought to have cured me of such naivete. Every day she shared with us her great and abiding obsession—how hard it was for our conduct to match our professional ideals. She put it in this unremarkable manner—drew upon, actually, a commonplace saying: "Try hard to practice what you preach." The first three words, of course, were her rather interesting modification of that old saying. She knew how difficult it can be for any of us, no matter how well intentioned, to achieve the lofty congruence of stated rhetoric with everyday behavior.

166

I recall the clever question of one of my young classmates; she asked Miss Avery one day whether those who *don't* preach really have any reason to be worried—since, after all, they are not hypocrites. Miss Avery was a bit surprised, I still remember, but she soon had thought out her response—to the effect that we are all preachers in our particular ways, and so there is no escaping the moral mandate of that aphorism, which she had put on a rather large piece of cardboard, pinned on the wall behind her desk. (Often she stood up, pointed at the words on the cardboard and asked us, as a class, to recite them!)

Those were the days when a teacher could read from the Bible in a public school classroom without the Republic's essential character being destroyed. I remember the various favorites of Miss Avery quite well—her love for passages from Isaiah and Jeremiah, and her love for Luke's version of the life of Jesus. I remember, too, the way she read the fourth chapter of Luke—the emphasis she put on that injunction Jesus calls upon, "Physician, heal thyself." She asked us what that meant, and we puzzled, and struggled with our answers, and slowly dared raise our hands to answer. She brought us closer and closer to the meaning—and then, as if a magician who had waited all along to show us her favorite trick, she picked up the pointer and with it directed our eyes to that large piece of cardboard with its familiar message. All roads lead to Rome, we began to realize!

The longer I live, the more grateful I am for such a fine teacher— for the unforgettable emphasis she persisted in giving to the enormous irony that shadows us throughout life: our capacity, our willingness even, and, alas, our stubborn determination, at times, to talk one line, live another. The more flagrant instances are memorable—the policeman who is caught stealing, the lawyer who breaks the law, the fireman who turns out to be an arsonist, the cobbler who can't seem to find time to repair his own children's shoes, and, again, the doctor who ardently heals his or her patients, and gives short shrift to his family and friends, or hers—not to mention the minister or priest or rabbi who thunders biblically on Saturday or Sunday, yet ends up betraying the Lord through violations of His various commandments.

There is a less dramatic version of this sad disparity between professed belief and concrete behavior—a version I fear many of us know all too well: the pious churchgoer who gossips discreetly, or gets a secret (pleasurable) rush of adrenalin upon learning of some-one's bad news; or the medical student, the physician who goes beyond conscientiousness and, in fact, feeds off the misery of his or her patients; or the psychiatrist who gets all too much personal satisfaction from the troubles of his patients—to the point that "treatment" becomes (as Freud put it) "interminable," so much that a dispassionate observer from another planet would, no doubt, wonder who is treating whom.

Such vexing examples of human frailty, if not evil, are part of this life; I imagine one can make too much of them. However, some of us are so protected by the idolatrous responses of our patients, clients, students, or parishioners that we lose sight altogether of that side of ourselves—the hypocrisies we enact in the daily course of our lives. We even have ideological maneuvers at our disposal— ways of dismissing others if they should be bold and sassy enough to point out our pretenses, our moments and longer of insincerity or (moral) inconsistency. "*He* has a problem!" "*She* is in obvious trouble!" The protection that such psychological deviousness offers us is considerable these days—all the dreary smugness one witnesses in clinics or in everyday conversations, as one or another person is trotted off to a psychological corner ("he needs help"), while the person who makes the judgments (using those cool, slippery, even-handed phrases that would be laughable if they weren't so per-suasive to so many of us) emerges as yet again triumphant.

It would be wonderful if St. Augustine's kind of confessional self-scrutiny (or that of St. John of the Cross in his *Dark Night of the Soul*) would obtain among more of us in these last few years of the 20th century. If such were to be the case, if more of us could be tougher with ourselves as self-observers, as self-critics, we might be spared some of the truly outrageous spectacles that keep coming our way: the terrible arrogance, for instance, of some of those who profess compassion for the poor and humble; and the radical greed-iness and selfishness of some of those who announce their loyalty to Washington and Jefferson and Lincoln and who claim to be born (or born again) Christians—meaning contemporary followers of a once obscure rabbi who spent his time with no one very important; and too, the tattling and whispering, the *ad hominem* psychological broadsides of those who claim to love their fellow human beings, or to be interested in understanding them, treating them, curing them.

"Physician, heal thyself," my fifth-grade teacher used to tell us—in such a way as to remind us, unforgettably, how small that distance is between what we dislike and what we want to see changed, on the one hand, and what is right there within ourselves, all too unrecognized, on the other hand.

November 1986

A Victim of Spiritual Poverty

I hope I never forget him, a 12-year-old boy in New Orleans whom I got to know in the 1960s, as that city struggled with the turmoil of school desegregation. But that child was white, went to a fancy private school, and was the much-loved son of extremely rich parents. No racial crisis bore down on him, as it did on the much more vulnerable white people of that interesting old port city, not to mention the blacks who lived there in such substantial numbers. The boy already had a sense of himself—"an air of importance about him," as one of his teachers put it. When I came to visit his parents, and hear what they thought—the father was an exceedingly influential lawyer who had taken a strong interest in the progress of school desegregation—the boy would inevitably appear, approach me, and tell me (whether I asked or not) what he had on his mind. Often his comments took the form of admonitions, caveats: didn't I know that "the colored" are not "reliable," or "don't always speak so you can understand them"? When I disagreed with him, or even gently challenged him, he got huffy: I'd find out, eventually, the truths he already knew.

I kept in touch with him over the years (the 1960s and 1970s) and I did find out certain truths—what it was that characterized much of his life. They were truths he was quite willing to share with me—as in this self-regarding series of observations, made when he had turned 16: "I hate these long spring vacations. We've been everywhere! We just keep going back to places! My mother likes to see those ruins in Mexico. My father likes to go out West and ski. They fight over where to go. I just like a swimming pool in a hotel, near the ocean, with lots of different restaurants and a good tennis pro. If I have my way, I'll be the best tennis player in the world. I'll play all the tournaments! I have a pro here, but he's not good enough. I think I'll outgrow him soon. I don't like tennis camps: too many people! I like a good game with a pro who knows how to teach, but isn't too pushy.

"I don't know what I'd like to do when I'm older. I wouldn't mind 'real estate development.' I'm not sure what it is, but I hear my father's friends say you can make two or three extra fortunes in it, if you're savvy. If you're not [savvy] you have no business in it [real estate development]. I don't just want to sit on my inheritance; I know that. You've got to keep your assets growing, or you'll slip back. There's always some dude coming down the pike, ready to shove you aside and take the lead! I'd like to be up there, out in front—that's my ambition!"

In his 20s he was no less determined to "keep up there," as he'd often put it. I had known him long enough to be able to joke with him, even push him hard about his ideals and values. He is a good-natured person, and quite generous to his friends. He is also practical, earthy, and in certain respects quite unpretentious—a contrast, I often realize, with some of us politically liberal academics, whose assertively declared compassion for others is all too evenly matched by our showy self-importance, and our gossipy delight in dismissing anyone who happens to have the slightest reservations about one or another of our chosen "causes." Not least, he has continued to be ambitious: "I'd like to get a new business going—something different from all others! I'd like to see my business grow and grow, and then I'll be way up there, and my friends will pick up a copy of *Fortune* or *Business Week* or *The Wall Street Journal* and they'll see me. You're only here once, and you have to prove yourself. If you don't, then it's your loss. If you don't, you have no right to be belly aching about someone who's gone and done something and got someplace. Why are people so mad, because a guy goes and makes himself a success out of life?

"You keep asking me what I want out of life, and I keep telling you—but you don't believe me! Things don't have to be as complicated as can be; they can be simple. You get an idea; you play with it, until it really makes sense; you figure out how you can go from point A to point B; you plan and plan about what you'll do then, when you're at point B—and then, one day, you take the plunge, you go for broke. If you fail, you fail: you take the blame on your shoulders and you don't weep and moan and start bemoaning everyone else. If you don't fail—if you succeed—then you take the credit, and you don't start apologizing to the world, because you've come out on top! No, sir! This country became what it is because there were people who had the courage and the toughness to take risks, and to keep pushing—to have dreams, and to work hard to make the dreams come true. If we keep apologizing because of our success—if we start losing our spirit, and feeling we're bad, because we want to be rich and have some influence in the world, then we'll become a different country. We'll all have the welfare mentality before long!"

I won't easily forget probing with him that phrase "the welfare mentality." He was tolerant of me and my worries—ready to explain himself. But he was not at all inclined to yield territory—including any of the higher ground of moral conviction: "When people think the country—the federal government, or the city—owes them a living, they've lost all their self-respect. They've become parasites. You may think we can afford to have a lot of people like that in the country, but the more we have, the bigger the burden, and soon you have a few working hard and millions sitting and doing nothing for themselves. That would be the end of America—a disaster for the world. It would be a terrible thing for the Christian religion, too. The Communists would swallow up Christianity. My idea of what Christianity should be [is] . . . each person standing there, alone, before God, and showing Him that you have the courage to live your life to the fullest, to do the best you can with the gift he's given you: the time to spend here."

I suppose many would want to become indignant, outraged by such statements, and for understandable reasons. Perhaps because I've known this person almost his entire life (and a big hunk of my own) I feel otherwise—saddened, even a little hurt: so much intelligence and energy which never seem to be offered to others, but rather, get channeled into the various real estate deals he's learned to make. He himself describes those "deals" as "speculating"—for him no pejorative word, any more than the mergers and takeovers we've been observing in recent years are, for him, suspect or worse. I suppose my anger toward him takes the form of pity. I lament the direction he has taken—hear myself calling him vulnerable, needy, virtually indigent: a victim of spiritual poverty who makes me realize how morally exalted, how spiritually affluent some materially impoverished people I've met have managed to become. "We have to pray for the lost souls we see among us," Dorothy Day used to say—and then she'd always add, "and hope that we won't become one of them." One prays; one hopes.

December 1986

Voluntary Poverty

All the time I used to hear Dorothy Day speak of "voluntary poverty," and then I would think of the many poor people I have known—their urgent and profound and continuing desire to break out of poverty, enjoy the various "goods and services" the rest of us manage to find available for ourselves. Once in a poor neighborhood of Boston I talked with some devoutly religious people about their circumstances; and having heard them hope (against hope) for a better time of it, and having heard them spell out that hope with a shopping list of sorts (what a release from poverty would mean in concrete terms), I took a deep breath and made a plunge: "There are some who would argue that possessions can rob us of our closeness to God. We forget Him because our minds are on what we want to buy, to own, day and night."

A man sitting opposite me didn't hesitate long before he began talking: "It must be wonderful to be in the position of worrying about the possessions you have! I've never gotten into that kind of situation, and I suspect I never will! If we get through one day, that's fine; we start worrying about the next day. If I had enough money so I didn't have to think about money all the time—well, that would be a great breakthrough for me! I doubt, though, that I'd start thinking that I was in a lot of trouble with God, just because I could take my next meal for granted, and the one after that, and so could my wife and kids.

"Now, maybe you know something we don't know! I've heard of the spoiled rich! But I don't think I'm in danger of becoming one of them—not just yet. It really gripes me—to tell you the truth—hearing people who've had it a lot easier than I have, tell the world that it's bad, and you're in danger before God, if you get too interested in food and clothes and money. When you're poor, you

have no choice—unless you want to hoist the white flag and surrender, starve to death maybe! It's nice that some people can turn
away from the comforts they've known, and then start telling the
rest of us that we should ignore 'material things,' and only pay
attention to God, and to the 'higher things.' When you were giving
us that rap, I thought to myself: does he really believe that for
himself, and even if he does, what does he think we do here, spoil
ourselves with fancy food and clothes and lots of vacations and lots
of buying and buying? We're not sure where our next dollar is
coming from—and then there are people who say give it all up, give
it all up! I'll bet they've never known 'poverty' the way we have—
and I'll bet when they give it all up, they still don't! I mean, they
know how to get by, and they know who to go to for help, if they're
really in a lot of trouble."

In a blunt manner he had put his fingers squarely on the utter,
rock-bottom reality of "class" as it comes to bear not only on the
everyday motions of our life, but on the assumptions we have with
respect to what is or is not likely or possible. As I heard that man
make those statements I thought of some of the reasonably well-to-
do and well-educated people I know who have made a point of
telling me, and others, how much they scorn the "crass materialism
of this culture" (as I recently heard it put, in a not completely
original way); how earnestly they hope to rid themselves of the
consumerist preoccupations so many others seem to have; how
fervently they would prefer an "alternative life style," if not (as one
person put it in a lecture I attended) a "life free of property
consciousness." When I asked what such a life would entail, I was
told that "voluntary poverty" was the person's aim.

Who would want to decry or wax sardonic at such an objective?
My wife has kept urging me to be grateful that there are those who
are interested in such a life's pursuit—and I guess I am, indeed,
grateful, more or less. Yet, I still remember what that ghetto man
said, and I know that some who advocate "voluntary poverty" will
never be as vulnerable as he, never be as close to the edge of things.
I remember, in this regard, Dorothy Day turning on her own plea
for "voluntary poverty" with the shrewd observation that she and
Peter Maurin, after all, were not exactly unable, even during the
worst of the Great Depression, to seek out help from others, and
obtain it. They were articulate; they had lots of friends, some not
exactly poor; they were blessed with like-minded colleagues who

were willing to seek far and wide on their behalf. The contrast with, say, the ghetto people who make up the involuntary poor, by the millions, of our cities is all too obvious.

I suppose I am trying to say that "voluntary poverty," in all its moral beauty, is still for many of us a privilege—and alas, can become a grave temptation to pride, if not distinct arrogance. The spectacle of some with a network of educated and well-to-do relatives insisting upon their scorn for "creature comforts" (another derisive phrase I sometimes hear) while themselves being able to count upon inherited money, discreetly set aside, or on all the advantages, tangible and intangible, that go with a "background" and an advanced "level of education" does not go unnoticed, I fear, by many who are "dirt-poor," with no likely chance of ever being otherwise. Meanwhile, of course, there are those who love to find and savor such ironies—clap their hands at the distance between the professed high ideals of some and the ongoing grim circumstances of others.

"There is poverty and there is poverty," a medical school classmate of mine used to warn me, as I did my stint at a Catholic Worker hospitality house—and I was furious at him for being so cynical (and arrogant, and self-serving) himself: a justification, I kept thinking (and still do) for his politics, his way of regarding the world, not to mention, living a particular (quite comfortable) life. Still, he had spotted a certain kind of pride at work in me—a measure of self-serving blindness. The more I denounced him and others like him in my head, the easier it was for me to avoid recognizing a condescending hauteur in myself: me, the one who extends himself to others, and me, the one who doesn't get caught in the self-indulgence of that "crass materialism." Good that I didn't; good that I try not to do so today—but how lucky and fortunate the life that has enabled such an outlook, such gestures. We ought keep our self-respect, and further, take the risk of being glad that we have found certain aspirations, certain ideals for ourselves—such as the hope of a life not given over completely to the passion of ownerships, to endless acquisitiveness; but we also need to remember that the struggle toward voluntary poverty is a privilege indeed—and requires constant self-scrutiny, lest a smugness and self-righteousness assert their authority and undo morally, yet again, a decent and honorable effort.

January–February 1987

On Forgiveness

Once, during an afternoon's conversation with Anna Freud (who founded the field of child psychoanalysis and who, during her long life, was ever attentive to her father's ideas and works) I was surprised to hear her bring up the subject of forgiveness. We had been talking about an elderly woman's long and troubled psychological history. Her son was a chronic schizophrenic of the catatonic kind—spells of serious mental deterioration, during which he was confused and given to incoherent thinking, talking, writing. This most serious of mental illnesses had begun in the son's adolescence, and had, in effect, crippled him for life. In his early 50s he was living a marginal life socially and economically—no matter the good education he had received as a youth, and the family's solid situation in society. The woman's husband had also developed a serious psychiatric illness: a depression took control of his life during his 60s, and never really relinquished its hold on him. (He died in his early 70s.) This man had been a psychologically solid and sensible person; he came from a family with no history of psychiatric troubles. A businessman, then educator, he had always been a decent, thoughtful, affable, conscientious, and quite eventempered person; but in his last years he became sullen, moody, increasingly remote and morose.

Meanwhile, the mother of that son, the wife of that man, spent her time pursuing all sorts of interests and activities connected, always, to the cultivation of herself—her mind, her hobbies, her "relationships." She was, alas, an extremely self-centered person, a case-history illustration for Christopher Lasch's *The Culture of Narcissism*. She was ever ready to connect anything and everything to her own thoughts and wishes. She was, in a way, a living caricature of the well-to-do, aged dilettante. She took yoga lessons. She took recorder lessons. She experimented with acupuncture. She drank a lot in secret. She collected gossip, and spread it in one flurry of letters after another. She attended funerals, and delighted in passing word of them to others. Most of all, she read psychology books, took psychology courses—and of course, went to a succession of "therapists" in the course of a long and rather earnest and persistent search for what she kept calling "insight." Unfortunately, she used her psychological interests—her scattershot and often naive, if not pitifully inadequate acquaintance with various theorists of "personality development"—in an especially destructive manner. She was always Mrs. Know It All—ready to explain someone's words, actions, interests, aspirations, invoking at every moment the authority of psychology and psychiatry. She was for many of her supposed friends a somewhat pathetic figure—a person whose son's illness and husband's illness had clearly marked her for life in a peculiarly modern manner: the parlor psychologist who deflected any possible thought in anyone's mind that *she* might be the most troubled person in her entire family by a constant readiness to interpret the other person's behavior or statements. Behind her back even those closest to her mocked her habits and recognized the craziness of her manner.

Miss Freud was no stranger, of course, to that kind of person, or to her way of dealing with her difficulties, her life. "She is the classical military tactician," she said, referring to the above described person's use of psychology. Miss Freud continued with further explanatory comments: "It is no surprise that this old widow [her husband had by then died] takes such pains to use psychology as her principal weapon. She spends lot of time figuring people out, applying psychiatric labels to them, trying to convince everyone how psychologically 'aware' and 'sophisticated' she is. She is what in America is called a 'pop psychologist.' She is really afraid that someone—lurking behind some corner of her life!—will figure her out, will stop and realize that this is someone who, after all, may well have had no small role in the severe mental illness which the two men in her life suffered. We used to hear a lot of discussion of the 'schizophrenogenic' mother, the mother who subtly and not so subtly drove her child crazy. And, of course, we know a wife can drive a husband crazy, and vice-versa. But the point is not to attribute blame by coming up with such interpretations, simply to try to comprehend why such and such a family turns out as it does.

This is a terribly hurt family we have heard described. It is not only 'split,' in that the two men in it were torn apart; the other children [three daughters] aren't all that close together, either. The family never comes together as a family. The old widow turns her attention to one, then the other; they each are asked to 'connect' to *her*, not to one another, not to something larger, to a greater family of children and grandchildren. It is as if the old grandmother is playing one off against the other; is afraid that if they all come together, they might find out something—about her. And what would they find out? What they each know, already I suspect—that underneath it all she is scared and, no doubt, ashamed of herself. In her dreams, in the middle of the night, alone with her thoughts, she may well be haunted by her awareness of her own considerable part in the mental collapse of the two men in her life. I suspect she is a brittle, angry person—and look: the son's catatonia and the husband's depression both tell of men utterly silenced. They must have sensed how sick she was, and so sacrificed themselves (through the silence of their illness) for her sake! Even her grandchildren stay away from each other—those in one family not knowing those in another. Meanwhile, she wraps herself in the aura of psychology, moves from each person to person, attends funerals, exchanges gossip—hides from her own loneliness and despair and guilt, I would guess."

With that sharp summary (only some of which I relate here) I thought we were through with yet another melancholy psychoanalytic look at a person, a family. But suddenly Miss Freud had an afterthought. She shuffled her papers. She coughed, took some water. She indulged an old habit, charming in its own unpredictable way—she moved the fingers of her right hand briskly through her hair, as if, thereby, setting the stage for her mind's further activity and a concluding surmise: "You know, before we say goodbye to this lady, we should wonder among ourselves not only what to think—we do *that* all the time!—but what in the world we would want for her. Oh, I don't mean 'psychotherapy'! She's had lots of that. It would take more years, I suspect, of psychoanalysis than the good Lord has given her just to get her past all her 'psychology': the way she guards herself from herself by setting herself up—for all the world to see—as an eager part-time (maybe we should say, half-baked!) 'psychologist.' But isn't that what so many do these days, especially in America, where 'psychology' is on so many people's minds? I will confess to you: when I was listening to all of this, I thought to myself that this poor old lady doesn't need us at all. No, she's had her fill of 'us,' even if she doesn't know it. She's been visiting one or another of 'us' for years, decades, as she has dealt with her son's troubles, her husband's, her own. What she needs, I thought, is *forgiveness*. She needs to make peace with her soul, not talk about her mind. There must be a God, somewhere, to help her, to hear her, to heal her—so I thought for a second! But I fear she'll not find Him! We certainly aren't the ones who will be of assistance to her in that regard!"

With that last sentence she stopped her wry, ironic commentary—a little surprised at herself, I thought, for her mention of God, of His forgiveness. I don't think she was announcing, at that moment, a religious conversion; but I do think that she had been given pause by a particular instance of human turmoil, hurt, suffering, and yes, deviousness and cruelty—and had found herself, unwittingly almost, transported from one world to another, from (as she indicated) the world of the mind to the world of the soul. When will some of us learn that not rarely such a movement is not without important, redemptive consequences—that on our knees, in prayer, we might at last find His forgiving smile, at last accept His reminder that we are but part of something (someone) much larger, rather than (through our minds) the be-all and end-all of this life?

March 1987

Tolstoy's *Anna Karenina*

It is not hard to understand why Dorothy Day was so taken with Tolstoy. His moral passion was evident even in his early writing (as an observer of war in *The Sebastopol Sketches,* as an observer of himself and others nearby, in the partly fictional, partly auto-biographical *Childhood, Boyhood, Youth*). She, of course, had read (and reread) *War and Peace, Anna Karenina,* not to mention the later Tolstoy of religious introspection and intense personal anguish *(Resurrection, The Kingdom of God Is Within You, Confession).* Like others before and after her, she struggled with Tolstoy, even as he never stopped struggling with himself—the various sides of his intellectual and ethical life which he wanted so hard to reconcile. "I have to be in a certain mood to read Tolstoy," I remember her saying (1970). She was not thereby making empty talk; nor was she unaware of the relationship a novelist can have to one's psychology. We choose whom to read in accordance with the particular subjectivity which happens to possess us at one or another moment—unless some professor is compelling us to cram a whole list of books down our nervous gullets.

Later during that discussion of Tolstoy, Dorothy Day concentrated her attention on *Anna Karenina:* "I hear people say it is their favorite novel, but I can't say that, because I get too upset whenever I go back to it, and I do, from time to time. Once I told a young man—he had been a graduate student in literature, and knew Tolstoy quite well—that the person Anna Karenina (she's always been that, to me, an entirely alive woman, not a character in a novel!) reminded me of myself in certain ways, to the point that I want to go to church, sometimes, as I'm reading about her, and get on my knees and pray to God, to keep helping me not become more and more like Anna Karenina! The man was shocked; he clearly didn't believe me. He was beginning to tell me how different I was, when I decided I had to change the subject. I couldn't bear to go into a long explanation of what I had in mind! Sometimes, when you're discussing a certain subject, you assume that the most important part of the exchange has to be a silent understanding between you and somebody else! As in prayer—when you sit and say nothing, but everything is in your heart, and you hope the good Lord is taking notice. With some people, you can dare hope that what is tacit will remain so! It's terrible, when someone wants to 'draw out' what is best left understood, but not spoken!"

She went on, not surprisingly, to compliment that young man in other respects; but she had made her point, and I wasn't about to put to her a few questions on *Anna Karenina* which had come to mind. Indeed, I felt a bit loutish as we sat there—at a minimum, a casualty of a psychoanalytic culture, not to mention a career shaped by tenets developed in Vienna during the first three decades of this century. Later, though, suitably by myself and without the effort of putting words down, I remembered the Anna Karenina I had met when I first read that novel, as a college student, and then the Anna I had met the second time around, when I read the novel during my psychiatric residency. They had been, for me, two different women: in college, a victim of passion, during the training I was getting in psychiatry, a victim of a "troubled life" or, as we also kept saying, world without end, "a neurotic conflict." I knew that when Dorothy Day thought about the Anna Karenina she knew, another mode of thinking and analysis was being summoned—even as recently, when I read *Anna Karenina* yet again, I found myself responding to a woman altogether different from the one whose measure I thought I'd taken rather carefully twice before.

My hunch is that Dorothy Day saw in Anna a reflection of her own pride, her own peculiar egoism—of a kind, by the way, that a beautiful woman (in our culture) so often risks having as a lifelong companion. Tolstoy may have known Anna the way he fearlessly (and much to his continuing discomfort) knew himself—the self-absorption which, step by step, may come to rule our lives. Beauty, talent, power, ambition, and, yes, in that last regard, even religious ambition, can fatally wound the mind's moral defenses, make us all too insensitive to others as we turn around in our dizzying whirl. Anna's deterioration of heart and soul (and the similar decline that

takes place in her paramour, Count Vronsky) was not inevitable—
hence the psychological "genius" correctly ascribed to Tolstoy, who
knew how banal, how morally and emotionally unchallenging, how
false to life, it would have been to present Anna as the necessary
victim of an instinct that brooked no resistance or a troubled early
life which finally had asserted its sovereign authority. Tolstoy knew
the emotions of childhood exceedingly well—better, really, than
Freud, who was not nearly his match as a keen watcher of the
young, but who handed over to the early years an unqualified
mightiness (in the hands of some, both deterministic and reductionist). No wonder we never hear about Anna's childhood. She is a
grown woman, a wife, a mother of a son she loves very much, and a
woman of great warmth, sensitivity, and considerateness when we
meet her—not one with a history of early disorder and sorrow, nor
one with a more recent story of turmoil or failure. Tolstoy lets us
get to know her and Vronsky (and their gradually accelerating
involvement with one another) not because he wants to be ana-
lytically dispassionate or "understanding," one suspects, but because he craved the expression, through his pen, of the awesome,
ambiguous, ironic nature of our existence: what befalls us ruinously
may have its origins in an initial stroke of fate or luck, which then
sets in motion possibilities or alternatives—and it is our decisions
with respect to them which account for what, later on and in
retrospect, can occasionally seem to have been a sudden, singular
tragedy, a crippling assault that came out of nowhere and sense-
lessly took all in its way.

Put differently, Tolstoy is at pains to give both Anna and
Vronsky free will, as God did for all of us. *Anna Karenina* is,
indeed, one of our greatest treasures precisely because its tragedy is
biblical (rather than contrived, cleverly arranged, or magically
foisted). Anna's "passion" (and Vronsky's, too) is pride—the self
fueling its inexhaustible appetite for new sources of expression, of
responsive engagement. Her husband's limitations are not her
"problem," any more than her son's radiant love for her is her
potential salvation. Tolstoy might have probed her psychology and
Vronsky's more insistently (he certainly knew how to do so), but he
goes only so far in that direction because he wants his adulterous
affair to be, alas, what such "love" not rarely can turn out to be—an
occasion for two individuals not so much to know one another as to

give vent to themselves. That is why the other major character in the novel, Konstantine Levin, so often described as a foil for Tolstoy's self-expression, is so intriguing: he, too, struggles with pride, with his own wounded vanity—but at a critical point he manages to take up arms against this most insidious and dangerous of antagonists, and emerges not without plenty of residual egoism, but with a grip on himself, so to speak: able sufficiently to subdue his self-preoccupations to make for a substantial contrast with Anna and Vronsky. By the skin of his teeth, it seems, he escapes their downward direction and destination—the margin many of us know to be the case in our own lives when we stop and think the matter over.

April 1987

Tolstoy's *Confession*

I remember reading *Confession* when I was in the second year of medical school, and immersed in the study of pathology and pharmacology. Neither of those two subjects was making much sense to me. I had yet to meet a patient, and the insistent factuality of everyday life, untethered to any human actuality, struck me as pointless, even perverse. My college advisor, Perry Miller, had pressed the essay on me repeatedly, but I had withstood his enthusiasm—perhaps because I sensed, from the way he talked, how scornful Tolstoy was, in that essay, of the intellectual life as so many of us (all too full of ourselves) end up living it.

The last thing I needed at that time was the encouragement I was tempted to take from Tolstoy—not necessarily the kind he intended to offer his readers. For me *Confession* threatened to be another reason to quit medical school and go find some work that might help me break out of the bonds egoism had put on my mind's limbs—hence my lack of interest. But I had been sent the book by a friend of mine who was having similar trouble making sense of the education he was pursuing—in his case, the source of misery was law school. If he could claim exhilaration after exposure to *Confession*, I was ready to take the risk.

I started reading the book late at night, after I'd submitted my brain to the usual lists of organ parts, and, too, the nomenclature of disease and death. I'd intended a relaxed 15 minutes of Tolstoy, followed by the deep sleep I'd been having regularly at that time in my life—my mind's way of saying it was more than happy to escape the educational reality that had prompted each evening's total absorption. But suddenly I lacked interest in sleep; I read until Tolstoy's *Confession* was ended; I put out the light and tried to doze; I tossed about; I decided to get up and go get a snack; I did; I

185

carried the book I'd been reading with me—though when I met some medical school students getting their snacks (we had an exam the next morning) I slipped the book into my overcoat. When I got back to my room, I started reading the essay once again. The next morning I did poorly on the test, not the first time such an event took place. I recall thinking I'd have done a bit better if we'd been asked to write on Tolstoy's *Confession*.

On the other hand, I might have had a good deal of trouble writing the kind of clever response many students like me learn to muster for our university examinations. It would have been hard to avoid being crippled by an awareness that my very essay was precisely what Tolstoy was scorning so strenuously in *his* essay—moral and spiritual issues turned into something "interesting," smart, or ever so shrewdly stated. Not that Tolstoy, even in this essay, hesitates to write persuasively—with flashes of the gifted story teller's inviting charm. But he *is* making a confession, and the result is a statement one finds hard to analyze—especially when, at a decisive moment, the author has this to say: "But as soon as I mixed with believers or picked up their books, a certain doubt, dissatisfaction, and bitterness over their arguments rose up within me, and I felt that the more I grasped their discourses, the further I strayed from the truth and the closer I came to the abyss."

His next words escalate the line of argumentation even further: "Many times I have envied the peasants for their illiteracy and their lack of education." He is not, of course, glorifying ignorance *per se,* but he knows the hazards of a skepticism fueled by the kind of caviling temperament any number of well-educated minds are trained to possess. Doubt becomes a kind of faith—and self-importance the posture of the doubter. Earlier in the essay he had made an interesting distinction: "Having failed to find an explanation in knowledge, I began to look for it in life, hoping to find it in the people around me." The explanations he sought were the ones we all seek, wittingly or no, to those utterly rock-bottom questions: what does this life mean, and how ought one live it?

Tolstoy began to observe men and women who were like himself. He acknowledges (talking about "confession") that the men and women he scrutinized were a special group, indeed: "I thought this narrow circle of learned, wealthy, and idle people to which I belonged comprised the sum of mankind and that the millions who had lived and continued to live outside of this circle were *animals*, not people."

He wrote those words in 1879, a decade after *War and Peace* had been published, and a short two years after *Anna Karenina* had appeared. He was by then 51 years old, perhaps the most respected voice in all Europe—and a man about to turn from the very salons in which he was held in such high esteem. Not that he hadn't sent earlier signals of the ethical introspection stirring him, and of the desire he felt to be with the peasantry—to learn from the world's poor and humble, as well as be their teacher (and spokesman). It is no enormous step from Konstantine Levin in *Anna Karenina* to the essayist of "Confession"; and the man who wrote the essay on history attached to *War and Peace* is already of a moral sensibility that would encourage long and deep looks inward.

Confession offers a sustained grappling with matters we in this century call "existential"—all described by a novelist eager to avoid the abstract, the theoretical, and get close to narrative description, as when he sets down the various responses members of the bourgeois intelligentsia often make when the prospect of soul-searching comes to mind:

> As I looked about the narrow circle of my peers I saw only people who did not understand the problem, people who understand it but drowned it in their intoxication with life, people who understood it and put an end to life, and people who understood it but out of weakness continued to live a life of despair.

The summary is not unlike Kierkegaard's in *Either/Or*—a knowing glance at how we manage to glide by and escape the challenge that consciousness and language present to us. We are the creatures who know about death, and with language can ask all sorts of moral whys—yet we are also the creatures who can fool ourselves in dozens of ways, and sometimes the smarter we are, and the more privileged our lives, the more artful our tricks and dodges.

For Tolstoy *Confession* was the beginning of a new (and painful) stretch of time—to end only in his death over 30 years later. He would never again be able to sustain the pitch of the two great novels which preceded that essay, though he would certainly give us some extraordinary moral lyricism ("The Death of Ivan Ilyich,"

"Master and Man," "Hadji Murat"). For me, back then in medical school, that night and other nights to follow, *Confession* was a companion—a testimony that I could make a bit my own as I tried to figure out what the intellect had to offer, and what it was not meant to address. Soon enough I met suffering men, women, and children who hadn't heard of Tolstoy, and who hadn't gone to college or medical school, and who were by no means saints (the danger of romanticizing various others must always be kept in mind), but who had a few moral lessons, a few moral examples to offer some of us who attended them while they fought for life and encountered death.

May 1987

Tolstoy's *Resurrection*

Among the hilltop beatitudes Jesus gave us, the one that clouds the distinction between transgressors and those who do the law's work has always attracted the interest of people who know the universality of sin and the irony, if not hypocrisy, that a person risks when he or she condemns others. Still, societies necessarily have laws; and too, there are degrees of sin. Obviously, for instance, the murderous thoughts we have toward others do not amount to the actual taking of someone's life—and it is such an actuality with which the law has to come to terms. Nevertheless, He warned us: "Judge not lest ye be judged," and so doing, wanted to give us much pause.

Certainly Tolstoy paid heed to that warning in *Resurrection*, his last full-length novel, published in 1900, when he was 72, with a decade of living left to him. The kernel of the story is as "simple" as that of any of the world's great pieces of fiction—an unsurprising irony around which all sorts of narrative sequences can be arranged: a count, named Nekhlyudov, called to jury duty, finds himself obliged to decide the guilt or innocence of a defendant, the prostitute Maslova, who years earlier had been a servant in his family's home, and whom he had seduced and gotten pregnant. She stands falsely accused of the murder of one of her customers. Not that the author is interested in savoring such a legal set of circumstances in order to remind us that "guilt" is everywhere and "justice" at best a necessary but inadequate approximation. The count, we learn, is an ostensibly privileged man who has high ideals, noble thoughts, artistic aspirations, and reformist passions, but is a victim of a crime altogether different from the kind ascribed to Maslova: a tenaciously unwitting egoism which has locked him into a melancholy solitary confinement.

Much has been made by critics of the autobiographical aspects of this novel—Nekhlyudov as Tolstoy; his wife, too, regarded such to be the case. Rather obviously, however, Nekhlyudov did not write novels, especially one as vigorously self-satirizing as *Resurrection* is, in part, of Tolstoy (a side of him, at least), and one satirizing well-to-do dilettantes and their supposedly earnest causes, interests, activities, which follow one another relentlessly.

If, then, we see Tolstoy in the essentially vain and shallow count of the early chapters, whose moral journey is the central motif of *Resurrection*, we had best think of this novel as a confessional one—thereby emphasizing the qualities that made Tolstoy the Tolstoy we admire so much, not only as a wonderfully knowing observer of life, but as a fearlessly probing self-observer who had the keenest eye out for his own serious flaws of character. At the very beginning of *Resurrection* he quotes from the well-known passage in Matthew: "And why beholdest thou the mote that is in thy brother's eye, but considerest not the beam that is in thine own eye?" This is a warning in the same moral vein as the one mentioned at the start of this essay, and it is a warning not at all overlooked by the Russian novelist count we have all come to know so well, because he did, indeed, focus long and hard on that "beam" Matthew remembers hearing the Teacher mention.

All of Tolstoy's novels are written with exquisite devotion to the small moments of everyday life. The larger ethical and intellectual matters which pressed constantly on his often feverish brow are never dropped suddenly, awkwardly, rudely, truculently in the reader's lap. In his fiction he was a moralist, alright, but gentle and insinuating, not a scold. He was a man who knew himself well, and dared arraign himself along with others—the Russian nobility, the Russian Church, and the functionaries who worked in government and law.

Who can pick up a novel titled *Resurrection* without going back some 2,000 years in time to a then obscure part of a mighty empire? Back then the One who preached, taught, healed, whom we now worship, made a point of spending his time with the kind of people who populate Tolstoy's last novel aplenty—made certain He kept company with peasants, with the sick and ailing, and not least, with those who had been rebuked and scorned by all the proper ones, even put into prison by them. His desire to reach out with compassion and love to those whom others would call immoral or criminal or a threat to civil or political or religious authority obviously had great significance (hence the charge that He was a criminal, and the state decision to impose upon Him the death penalty). Tolstoy, at the very start of this century of ours, refused to forget that ancient social and legal paradox: God's chosen life with not only the poor, but with outcasts and the condemned, and the nature of God's death at the hands of the law, with criminals to His left and right.

Who is to decide what we ought emphasize with respect to the life of Jesus, and with respect to His words, His manner of being— and for what reasons? Of course, we do so all the time—we who lack the kind of moral intensity Tolstoy had in the last years of his life, as he tried (and inevitably failed somewhat) to take the life of Jesus seriously. We overlook what He said or did on the grounds of our own values, on the grounds of what suits us, is practical, works in this modern age—and maybe we protect ourselves from our own potential unease or the reprimand of others by calling a Tolstoy an eccentric, a man with "serious psychological problems," or in a more complimentary dismissal, a genius with an impossibly demanding and confusing way of trying to live.

Tolstoy's genius is doubted by no one, but his importance as a moral visionary has earned him less respect by all to many of us. We are apt to forget the direct line from him to Gandhi (who admired him so much and learned from him and corresponded with him) and thence to Martin Luther King Jr., who depended so much on Gandhi's teachings, and who, I well remember, mentioned Tolstoy often in conversations. As a matter of fact, I still remember when a few of us talked with him about *Resurrection,* which he had not read, and described to him the novel—its account of a man's progressive confrontation with his own smugness, selfishness, thoughtlessness; its account of his effort to change; the skepticism with respect to his strength of character expressed by Maslova; and, very important, its account of the determination, the toughness, the penetrating perspicacity of the downtrodden.

Dr. King was both extremely interested and sad—the latter because he knew how little time he had for a fairly long novel, given his own moral struggle, and too, his struggle with the law. "One day," he said softly, he hoped to read that novel, and others in its tradition. Meanwhile, the rest of us are left with the time denied him; and left with the continuing presence of Tolstoy's *Resurrection* among us—which meant to show how difficult it can be, even for a reasonably well-intentioned person of some moral sensibility, to change old, solipsistic habits. In the end, shaken and taught by Maslova's moral realism and moral intelligence, Nekhlyudov seems considerably more reflective—a step toward a new life, hence the book's title, with its reminder that such a possibility has been given us, though whether we care to take notice is another question.

June 1987

Two Tolstoy Stories

Tolstoy's admirers and critics have many times pointed out the significance of his religious crisis for his fiction. Nothing he wrote afterwards would approach the grandeur of *War and Peace* and *Anna Karenina*. Some push the matter further, telling us that novels written by moralists such as Tolstoy in the last three decades of his life never really work because their didactic intentions (the wish to convert the reader to one or another point of view) inevitably undermine "art."

Of course Tolstoy is being held, in this regard, to the highest standards. Those two novels, arguably, in their sum, offer fiction of a quality never before or after equalled. Even had Tolstoy's later life been calm and untouched by moral and psychological tempest, he might not have been able to give us a third story that would be a fit companion in stature to those giant novels. Moreover, what we love about them is the visionary side, as it connects with the particulars of various incidents and events. That is, Tolstoy's religious sensibility was at work long before he had his well-known "crisis," and that sensibility informs both *War and Peace* and *Anna Karenina*. In any event, as we think of the religiously agitated Tolstoy, who even dismissed his earlier work (those two novels!), we understandably feel "art" a victim of a writer's "life"—thereby heightening yet again a certain distance demanded between the two by any number of literary essayists. To be sure, "art" will naturally draw upon or respond to the "life," we acknowledge—but it has to have its own protected territory.

Yet, Tolstoy's "The Death of Ivan Ilych" was written in his late 50s, in the midst of his religious crisis and "Master and Man" appeared in 1895, when he was in his late 60s and, by his own inflammatory statements in the essay "What is Art," at a passionate remove from the aesthetic point of view with respect to literature which any number of his critics uphold as a matter of course. In that essay he insists that art ought to provide a moral life—become, functionally, rhetoric or propaganda, some readers understandably conclude. Still, from a turbulent and aging mind and from a pen explicitly dedicated to ethical instruction came two stories which are themselves full of turbulence, and do indeed instruct—and yet, also, possess in abundance the traditional requirements of "art": the beauty and guile and indirection and openness to interpretation which a more aesthetic criticism demands.

When I was an intern I worked with a distinguished cardiologist whose patients, not rarely, were similarly prominent men and women. I recall even now one such individual, a lawyer who had been a judge, then had resigned to return to the law. He was dying of an especially painful and fast-moving cancer, lodged in his esophagus and moving assertively to other parts of his body. One morning, taking his blood for tests I knew to be of no real use to him or any of us (doctors and their need to show their continuing effectiveness and authority, if not magical powers!), I heard him say what I was thinking: "I will soon be dead, so why bother?" I was grabbing hard for responsive words, with no success, when he changed the subject abruptly with another question: "Have you ever read that?" His head pointed in the direction of his bedside table, on which, beside a box of Kleenex and a dish meant to receive his spit and vomitus (there was plenty of the latter), I spotted a book: a selection of Tolstoy's stories. I said yes, I'd read some. He asked if I'd read "The Death of Ivan Ilych." Yes, I had. What did I think of it? Oh, it was a great story—the usual banal words meant to signal a willingness to tarry only so long over an essentially passing moment or short-lived exchange. But the patient had another intention in mind—or maybe, had surrendered to other demands at work in this universe. When I had finished with the tourniquet and syringe and needle, he leaned over, picked up the book, opened it to the Ivan Ilych story, read me a few lines, and then, all of a sudden, burst into tears.

This was a tough, self-possessed, taciturn lawyer whose cool, somewhat haughty, and even arrogant manner had up until then put me off considerably—another big-shot patient of my big-shot "attending," as we interns called one or another of our bosses. Now I was really speechless, and in a way, confronted with myself as well as with him and his changed behavior. What to think not only of him, but of my confident and unqualified estimate of him? Within moments he had pulled himself together—excused himself, but also given me a terse explanation: "You read a story like this and you can't help identifying with what you're reading." "Yes," I said quickly—and soon enough had excused myself, left the room.

Now I teach the story at a medical school, and am always impressed by its power to take hold of young, would-be physicians. It is a story that turns things around, examines a sequence, not of life, then death—the sequence we assume is everyone's fate—but rather of death, then life. For Ivan Ilych is presented to us not only as dead when the story opens (his physical death is announced right off) but as a cold, austere, ambitious, calculating lawyer and judge who has been "dead" all his life, or maybe, has never been "born." It is this person who falls ill, and will endure a slow, painful demise, in the course of which we see how sadly isolated and constricted his so-called life, with all its successes, has really turned out to be. As a human being, as a husband and father, as a professional man, he has lacked the virtues which in their day-to-day expression make for real life: thoughtfulness toward others, a willingness to give of oneself, considerateness—all the words and phrases we use to describe aspects of the love which had so obviously not informed Ivan Ilych's days and nights.

In the last moment of his life, however, he is wondrously "born"—is able to open up his mind and heart to others, accept them as he never had before; thereby he becomes alive, finally. Such a transformation is achieved by a writer who takes all the risks of sentimentality and banality, and instead, offers a story that is original, lively, arresting, and not in the least maudlin or dramatically forced—a story that shows the best of Tolstoy's narrative skill at work. A dying man who has pushed everyone away from himself emotionally becomes close to his young servant Gerasim, close to him physically as he is attended by the youth, but in time responsive to him, aware of him as a fellow human being, with his own worth and dignity—a comrade in life, so to speak. It is such an awareness that Ilych all along has lacked, and it is such an awareness that brings life to this man about to die. His son and wife come into his eyes—for the first time, really; they reach him, touch him. His heart has opened, even as it is ready to stop. A "light" descends upon him—and newly alive, he leaves the death of a life.

Even as Gerasim has been the instrument of this moment of salvation, the "man" in another Tolstoy story, "Master and Man," is also a servant, Nikita, whose businessman boss, Vasilii Brekhunov, has all sorts of plans and schemes and strategies. What Brekhunov wants is money, more and more of it, and influence. He swaggers. He is impatient with everyone, including those close to him. In a provincial 19th-century Russian setting, Tolstoy gives us man in search of mammon, at all (personal) costs. The story reaches its climax in a terrible winter storm, as the master and his servant, through the exertions of a horse named Dapple, are taken on a trip that is supposed to result in a successful and rewarding business deal. Brekhunov's greed prompted the trip, and as it unfolds, the servant and we the readers begin to realize what has happened— these two and their horse are prisoners of a fierce, unrelenting, blinding blizzard which shows no sign of ever loosening its grip. Brekhunov has a chance to escape; they can spend the night in warmth and safety at an intermediate place; but no, he wants to get to his proposed assignation as quickly as possible. He has lost all his judgment as he dreams of the money he expects to make.

The outcome is predictable: the master is in a winter's hell, and as lost as any character in Dante's *Inferno*. They go in circles, get nowhere—or rather, get closer and closer to death. The stoic endurance of the horse is tenderly, knowingly evoked—yet another animal who suffers the stupidities of his master, a so-called "civilized" creature known as a "human being." Nikita, the servant, also complies—aware that he is caught between the devil, as it were, and the "deep sea" of snow and a driving, tireless wind and sub-zero temperatures. Soon the three are stopped altogether. The horse stands there, dignity intact, awaits the end. The servant is similarly acquiescent, and touchingly reflective: so it goes in this hard life. The master has been wild with his determination to keep going and save himself at all costs—and to the devil with anyone else. But he can't save himself—the point of the story: can't do so either literally or in the metaphoric sense. He is "saved" by what happens to him in relation to his servant near him. Vasilii realizes that the one thing he can do before he dies is to put his body, still warm, on that of his servant Nikita. It is this gesture of concern for, appreciation of another which is Tolstoy's moral point, and which he works into a story indescribably compelling, poignant, touching. As in "The Death of Ivan Ilych," a greedy egoist just barely escapes a lifelong "death"—is "born" right before he dies—through circumstances that enable a last-ditch moral rescue.

These two Tolstoy stories tell us of life's redemptive possibilities; remind us that those who by secular standards have a lot can be in terrible spiritual jeopardy, and indeed, can be spared Hell only through the mediation of a humble one, even as Jesus Himself lived a humble life; and finally, insist that the time we have here is never over until the very end, no matter the various (psychological and sociological) determinisms, the stages and phases and complexes of various theorists who would have us marching like automatons through life. The book of our lives is open—even until the last breath. With these haunting tales Tolstoy admonishes us—but also invites us—to risk the saving grace of brotherly love, an opportunity for which may fall upon us out of nowhere, it seems, and enliven us in preparation for that last and most important journey to meet our Maker.

July–August 1987

On Politics

When I was a boy and youth I didn't know or care much about politics, perhaps because my parents had little use for the subject. They made a point of telling my brother and me that what really mattered were novels and poems; that politics had to do with lies and betrayals, whereas literature offered truth, a vision of what is good and honorable. Later in my life I would realize how hermetic, if not self-serving such a posture was—a way for them, alas, to distance their comfortable and privileged life from a kind of self-scrutiny that might have compelled the realization that their good fortune was itself the product of a certain kind of (materialist, bourgeois) politics.

Not that they didn't make clear to us how they voted, and their reasons for doing as they did. In fact, happily married as they were, they almost always differed in their political choices. My father was a Republican who regarded Robert Taft as his political hero. For dad the Republican party meant honesty in government, a respect for the rights of the individual. He saw the Democrats as crooked and corrupt, and since he lived in Massachusetts, he had plenty of reasons (in the 1940s and 1950s) to believe so locally. My mother, in contrast, voted Democratic, because she worried about the poor, about people she always described as "needy." The Republicans, she argued, care about "high principles" (how I remember her using that phrase!) but don't give a damn about the down-and-out. The Democrats, many of whom were admittedly crooked, nevertheless reached out to those who, she believed, required a helping hand, a boost up.

They were both aware, of course, that they had simplified matters—that the Republicans, too, can come up with crooks, *or* offer us humane leaders who try to help the poor, and that the Democrats can offer us leaders of the highest principles, men and women who believe in and try to uphold necessary and important political and moral virtues. Still, the way they sorted things out impressed certain distinctions in my mind, and they came to its surface as I thought about this symposium's subject. My father was a decent and quite generous man who had a profound distrust of consolidated political power—and its potential dangers and corruptions. English born and raised, he revered the parliamentary tradition, and like millions of others watched Europe go amok during the 1930's in the name of fascism and communism. He was suspicious, too, of bureaucracies, statist ones and also those in our large corporations. He loved dearly the checks and balances of the American system. (He came here as a young man to go to MIT, and stayed, having met my Iowa-born mother.) The one aspect of our political system he increasingly disliked was the modern presidency, with all its royalist susceptibilities, both in the minds of those elected to the office, and the rest of us, who vote in these sometimes odd creatures, the incessant sight and sound of whom we then have to endure four years at least. He especially had been disgusted by Franklin Delano Roosevelt's effort to pack the Supreme Court, as my mother used to remember in later years—and for good reasons. I mention that episode now for my own reasons: the constant dangers to a democracy—even in the name of humane reforms (the New Deal), badly needed. Even my mother, who loved FDR, was taken aback by that episode. In recent years, she, too, had worried about the inherent "sinfulness" of anyone as it gets connected in a life to an institution such as the modern presidency.

As I remember my mother and father, and recall the social and political issues which they considered important, I realize that I am still very much their son. My mother's Christian outlook, the readiness on her part to use a word like "sinfulness" in the midst of a political discussion, reminds me how flawed even our best intentions become. I wonder, then, whether a statist kind of socialism will not all too readily turn arbitrary, mean-spirited, abusive in many ways. At the same time, I have little love for the secular, consumerist world of contemporary America, so thoughtfully described by such social or literary observers as Robert Bellah, Mary Gordon, Christopher Lasch, Walker Percy. I loved Dorothy Day's mix of (the Catholic Worker tradition) moral traditionalism and radical egalitarianism—the latter tempered by a spirit of political tolerance one doesn't always find in strongly reformist cadres. Yes, the notion of a Christian socialism sounds attractive—but I truly wonder what would happen to those who became critical for the best of reasons and spoke out in a socialist world maintained by state power. My political heroes—Dorothy Day, Ignazio Silone, George Orwell, Danilo Dolci—have all had their good reasons to doubt not only fascist or communist totalitarianism but any socialist political system that couldn't be promptly voted out of office—meaning one to which there is a vigorously skeptical or critical political alternative or opposition.

I find myself often at odds with the social and cultural values of American liberals, not to mention radicals. I think, all in all, I am a social conservative, a political liberal, an economic populist or egalitarian—much as Daniel Bell once described himself. I try to connect all of those inclinations to my religious life, no easy thing to do at a time when so many priests, ministers, rabbis seem to attend the phrases of pastoral counselling, the junk talk of the social sciences, as if they are God's chosen words.

It's probably no accident that I keep going back to Simone Weil, and to Bernanos and Mauriac as well. They were conservatives with respect to family life; they upheld the importance of religion, of the Christian faith in our lives—and their hearts went out to those who suffer, who are poor and vulnerable, even as the heart of Jesus did.

I concluded with a sense of perplexity—as to what I ought say, recommend, espouse. In this country, at this time, I yearn for a kind of populism that would espouse traditional family values along with a vigorously reformist politics aimed at redressing the serious injustices which still obtain in this country. I wish our religions could be of help, in this regard—with ideas and values, energetically espoused—but so much of American religion, (namely all three major faiths) is sadly in awe of secular power, the secular culture.

October 1987

Teaching and Learning, Strutting and Conniving

These chapters have all been published under the same common title of "Harvard Diary," and yet as the reader will no doubt have noticed by now, after five or so years I haven't been all that interested in writing much about the place where at least some of my work (the teaching I do) takes place. I've mentioned occasionally what I teach, the novels I love, the writers whose words and values have meant so much to me. But what of the students I meet year after year in class after class? Although I am a pediatrician and a child psychiatrist, and took psychoanalytic training as well, I don't do much teaching in those fields, other than to supervise, occasionally, some hospital residents who are learning to work with children. Almost all my teaching time at Harvard is spent using novels and poems and short stories and occasional essays to explore moral or religious questions. I teach two undergraduate courses, one titled "A Literature of Social Reflection," the other "A Literature of Religious Reflection." In the former, we read writers such as Dickens, George Eliot, Hardy, Ralph Ellison, William Carlos Williams, Flannery O'Connor, Walker Percy. The thrust of the course is toward the question of conduct: how ought I live this life? The novelists who take a close look at the world usually have an idea or two about its rights and wrongs, and their way of seeing things morally can be a helpful antidote to the rhetorical or the analytic approaches—the preaching of the clergy (not to mention various secular scolds) or the abstract pronouncements of philosophical theorists. Stories address and evoke concrete experience, and can inspire in the reader a mimetic, an empathic response: the psychological and moral imagination awakened. We explicitly encourage

201

discussion of a central issue in moral philosophy and moral reasoning courses—how does one move from an intellectual analysis of ethical issues to a life that is honorable and decent? We also encourage students to be involved in volunteer activities—tutoring children, working with the sick, the elderly, the homeless—*and* we discuss in weekly sections their experiences in such activities, trying to connect the students' reading to the actions. A story such as Flannery O'Connor's "The Lame Shall Enter First," in that regard, can be a great moral prod of sorts—an encouragement for students and teachers alike to look inward at pride in the Biblical sense, the smugness and arrogance that sometimes we try to pass off as well intentioned intelligence and compassionate dedication at work. We hope that the combination of active involvement in the world outside the university and the vigorous self-scrutiny to which some of our best story-tellers submit themselves and their readers will, perhaps, make an actual difference in ongoing lives.

The course that takes up religious matters aims not to do so through theology, or religious philosophy or the study of history. We try to explore the subjective side of things by reading poems, essays, stories, autobiographical statements—*The Dark Night of the Soul,* by John of the Cross, Bonhoeffer's prison letters, Simone Weil's personal essays, some of Emily Dickinson's poems, selections from St. Augustine, Thomas à Kempis, the Silone novel *Bread and Wine,* Dorothy Day's *The Long Loneliness,* Georges Bernanos's *The Diary of a Country Priest.* To talk about those books with students is to be brought face-to-face, yet again, with those moral challenges long ago put to mankind by a then relatively obscure rabbi, as he walked through Galilee. "It's a little harder, with Bonhoeffer in your head, to make the usual phony excuses to yourself," a student remarked in a paper two years ago, and I often remember his words as a challenge to all of us—that we try to become a little less likely to betray ourselves morally with our mind's various strategies.

I love teaching students a bit further along—attending graduate school—and also use with them various novels, poems, short stories. I do so with medical students, law students, business school students. The hope is that a story by William Carlos Williams or Chekhov about the ethical choices and burdens with which doctors must contend—or the portrayal George Eliot gives of Dr. Lydgate's sad, moral decline in *Middlemarch*—will prove to be provocative in the better sense of the word: prompt all of us in a seminar room to think about our purpose in life, our assumptions and values. With law students I use the wonderful novels of Dickens—those in which lawyers prominently figure as agents, really, of a great writer's moral examination of a particular profession: *Bleak House, Great Expectations, A Tale of Two Cities*. We also read *Little Dorrit* for its close look at the various kinds of imprisonment (corporeal and spiritual) we in recent centuries have learned to impose on one another. The course is titled "Dickens and the Law," but addresses, really, the broader question of "the letter and the spirit" which St. Paul emphasized in that well known part of his second letter to the Corinthians.

At Harvard's Business School I also try to prompt such existentialist considerations through novels in which businessmen themselves confront such matters: William Carlos Williams's so-called Stecher trilogy *(White Mule, In the Money, The Buildup)*, the story of an immigrant family's rise to wealth and power; Walker Percy's *The Moviegoer*, whose central character, Binx Bolling, is a twenty-nine-year-old stockbroker who is more adrift morally than he can bear fully to know; F. Scott Fitzgerald's stories, of course—*The Great Gatsby, The Last Tycoon*, and a shorter one, "The Rich Boy"; Saul Bellow's *Seize the Day*, with its melancholy and tormented commodities trader Tommy Wilhelm; and not least, John Cheever's touching, haunting stories of success and disappointment both, of conceit and deceit, alas, as such human achievements and flaws take place in mighty Manhattan and its various environs. We all get more than a little perturbed by these fictions which tell so much about the moral facts of our lives—we who are "first" and so may well be in danger of ending up "last," a chronology remarked upon some two thousand years ago.

All that teaching and learning can be quite heady, though all one hopes for, really, is that the heart's motions be invigorated. Meanwhile, we are in continual jeopardy—of a kind I think best described once by a woman I knew who worked as a food server in a Harvard dormitory, and later, a waitress in the august Harvard Faculty Club. Unlike Flannery O'Connor, she had no expert knowledge of peacocks, but she could take the measure of her fellow human beings in a fairly sharp manner, I gradually realized. Once, when talking about Harvard, she mentioned all the teaching and learning that take place there, and took pains to emphasize the importance and value of such achievements. But she saw a darker side to the life around her at work, which she once described to me this way: "I see lots of good folks here, kids trying to learn all they can, and teachers trying to teach the best they can; but there's lots of big-shot, stuffed shirt folks here, and boy, do they sell themselves hard, and boy, do they do lots of strutting and conniving, and boy, are they the worst to go near and try to serve." She'll never write an article or a book, or a monthly column for a magazine, but all of us in Cambridge and other such high and mighty places the world over might try remembering the lesson she has learned about us as we contemplate the place where we are, the life that we are living, the destination we hope someday to achieve.

March 1988